**BE'ER HAGOLAH INSTITUTES**
671 LOUISIANA AVENUE
BROOKLYN, NEW YORK 11239

*"I did not come to this country to save myself or to seek positions of personal power,"* Rabbi Kotler said. *"Rather, I am here so that, with your help, we can save our brothers and the centers of Torah learning all over Europe!"*

*"On the other side of the ocean our brothers are waiting for our help,"* he continued. *"Only you, the Jews of America, are able to help them. Do it now! Save them!"*

Harav Aharon Kotler *zt"l*

In our generation, thousands of Russian children are landing on American shores each year. And it is now up to us to make the sacrifices.

Be'er Hagolah Institute was founded over a decade ago to combat the forces that were preventing the ideals of Judaism from reaching the *neshamos* of these innocent children.

There are presently over 1000 students studying at our school. This number is increasing dramatically each year as a result of the tremendous influx of new Soviet immigrants. Be'er Hagolah's outstanding staff of teachers, guidance counselors, family educators, and professionals offer a full range of educational programs for the students and their parents, as well as social experiences such as family *shabbatonim, chavrusa* programs with *bnei yeshivah*, Big Sister-Little Sister, Bais Yaakov programs, summer camping and countless other activities; all geared to introduce and inspire them to Torah living.

*"Each generation must answer to a different test. Our generation will have to give testimony regarding what we did for Russian Jews."*

Harav Yaakov Kaminetsky *zt"l*

# BE'ER HAGOLAH STUDENT WINS STATEWIDE ESSAY CONTEST!

Chana Polischuk
1402 Ave. K, Brooklyn, NY

Be'er Hagolah

## I'm Proud to be a Jew

"What is Klal Yisroel?", you may wonder. It's a group of people who are always together. That's right. The בני ישראל! From the time of מצרים over 3,000 years ago & until now, they remained together. I'm very proud to be part of that unity.

Anytime someone needs help, a Jew is always there. Because that's what a Jew is for—to help other Jews. After all "כל ישראל ערבים זה בזה."

I'm proud to be a Jew and serve 'ד by doing the 613 מצוות, even though it's hard to do the מצוות at my house because my parents aren't doing them. I still feel proud and will remain a faithful Jew no matter what. My teachers, friends, family and I myself are part of Klal Yisroel and we're doing a great job so far and it will continue on and on, no matter what and no matter where!

# AMERICAN
# ★DREAMS★

### The Story of a
### Jewish Immigrant Family

★ ★ ★

## SIDNEY R. LEWITTER

**Bristol, Rhein & Englander**
Lakewood, New Jersey

Published and distributed in the U.S., Canada and overseas by
C.I.S. Publishers and Distributors
180 Park Avenue, Lakewood, New Jersey 08701
(908) 905-3000 Fax: (908) 367-6666

Distributed in Israel by C.I.S. International (Israel)
Rechov Mishkalov 18, Har Nof, Jerusalem
Tel: 02-518-935

Distributed in the U.K. and Europe by C.I.S. International (U.K.)
89 Craven Park Road, London N15 6AH, England
Tel: 81-809-3723

Book and cover design: Deenee Cohen
Typography: Nechamie Miller
Cover illustration: Francis McGinley

ISBN 1-56062-262-8
Library of Congress Catalog Card Number
94-70749

PRINTED IN THE UNITED STATES OF AMERICA

THIS BOOK IS DEDICATED TO
THE MEMORY OF

MY FATHER
SHIMON NAFTALI LEWITTER

AND MY MOTHER
FAIGE CHANA LEWITTER

WHO THROUGH THEIR STRONG COURAGE, DEEP LOVE
AND CLEARLY FOCUSED RELIGIOUS FAITH, MANAGED TO
INSTILL IN ME FEELINGS OF THE ALMIGHTY THAT
COULD SURVIVE THE TURBULENT TRANSITION OF
JEWISH LIFE FROM EUROPE TO AMERICA.

# P R E F A C E

★

*American Dreams* tells the story of the Lewitter family, who came to America in the early part of the twentieth century. My father, Shimon Lewitter, was part of the tremendous influx of Jews from Eastern Europe to the United States between 1880 and the beginning of World War I. After the war, he brought his family to America. He came from Skalat, which was then part of the Austro-Hungarian Empire and became part of Poland between the First and Second World Wars. Today, it is within the new Ukrainian Republic.

*American Dreams* is, for the most part, autobiographical, although the book does contain some elements of fiction. There exists gaps in our family history which I had to bridge by the judicious use of imagination in order to present the probable lives of the Lewitter family. Nonetheless, I assure the reader that a consistent effort was made to create the fiction as logical realities of the times. If they were not true with the Lewitters, they were events that happened to other Jews in a similar time and place. Thus, if a label need be applied to the book, I would call it a docudrama, in the sense that it is a dramatized documentary of a fairly typical immigrant experience, based on my own family model.

I have used the third person form in telling the story of my family in order to gain objectivity. I have taken the liberty of assigning a modified surname to my family to compensate for some of the liberties I have taken with our family history. The name Halevy was not arbitrarily chosen. We are a family of Levites, and the names Halevy and Lewitter probably have a common origin. I have also taken the liberty of assigning different given names, surnames and character traits to some of the family members and acquaintances portrayed in this book.

I am the Joshua Halevy of the book, and that name is possibly closer to my real name than is Sidney Rubin Lewitter. I was named Reuven Joshua at birth, and my mother called me Sheyah, which proved difficult to use. I renamed myself Sidney, when I grew old enough to know how to handle that problem.

It is my hope that this story will provide some background for the development of the overall Jewish community during the first half of this century. We are all the children of immigrants, and we should seek to discover our recent American past in order to understand how we grew into what we are today and what our role as Jews should be in the present and future.

Many of the small details that give life its rich textures tend to be forgotten with the passage of time, and these details are usually not recorded in history. The colors and flavors of the times became lost to posterity. In *American Dreams*, I have tried above all to capture some of these flavors and preserve them for posterity. I have tried to paint a picture of the lifestyles, the poverty, the endless struggles, the fortunes and the triumphs as they existed in the vivid memories of my childhood and in the stories I heard from my parents about the old country. It was a world very different from the world of today, especially for the impoverished immigrants, but on the other hand, the promise of a boundless future was far more palpable in those days than it is today.

Through the experiences of my own family I have tried to show the varying degrees of assimilation among the immigrants—from those who never bothered to bring their *tefillin* to America to those who brought them but gradually forgot about them to those who wore them faithfully but did not bother to provide any for their American-born children. Most of these people had a simple, unsophisticated and rather superficial attachment to their ancient heritage, and they were not strong enough or motivated enough to fight for it in the bubbling cauldron of America. Tragically, therefore, too many of our people abandoned their religion while pursuing the American dream. But the passage of generations has dissipated the frenzy of the immigrant madness, and it is time to take a new and hard look at what they accomplished and the price they paid for it. There certainly is an American dream to be followed in this blessed and wonderful country, but it is not quite the same dream that dazzled and blinded our immigrant ancestors.

Finally, this book also adds a certain perspective to our perception of the holocaust. There were approximately ten years between the immigration of the Lewitter family to America in 1922 and the rise of Hitler to power in Germany in 1932. The same European anti-semitism that ultimately brought about the holocaust was already strong enough to cause Faige and Shimon Lewitter to flee Skalat.

I owe thanks to many people who have helped me to write *American Dreams*. Foremost is C.I.S. Publishers, who saw merit in the manuscript and caused it to be published. Rabbi Yaakov Yosef Reinman, one of the executives of the company, is truly a remarkable person. He is very intelligent, acutely aware of the intricacies of his profession as a publisher and yet his mild demeanor is completely consistent with that of a rabbi in Israel. It was a pleasure for me to work with him. I want to thank the editor of my manuscript, Mrs. Sarah Lehmann, who had to spend long, lonely hours in her work.

I thank Dr. Carl Calander, professor of creative writing at Brookdale Community College, for the help that he has given to me in the early stages of the book. I thank Leonard Mathless of the Yale University Library for his helpful guidance and advice. I want to thank Rabbi Tobias Roth of Congregation Brothers of Israel, Long Branch, New Jersey, for the help that he has given me. I also want to thank my very good friend Zev Berger for the help that he has given me in all of my writings by guiding me in the use of the computer.

My immediate family helped me enormously. I want to thank my brothers, Mr. Kenneth J. Lewitter and his wife Ruth, Mr. Morris Lewitter and his wife Sydell, and my sister Mrs. Lila Lewitter Hersh. We grew up poor, busy and happy. My brothers and my sister helped me remember some of the intricacies of our lives. I am happy that we had the opportunity of going over our past together.

I want to thank my cousin, Zev Reuveni, his wife, his daughter Nerd and his son Zvi for their important contributions to the manuscript. Mr. Reuveni is a resident of Petach Tikvah, Israel. He is the son of one of Shimon's sisters and therefore my first cousin. Zev Reuveni is a holocaust survivor, one of the very few of our family that numbered in the hundreds, who survived the war. He is a scholar and an educator whose vivid recollections of Skalat were very interesting and important.

I also want to thank David Shapiro, his wife and his brother Kalman who are also holocaust survivors. They are the children of Faige's brother Eliyahu and now live in the United States.

Their descriptions of the horrors of war know no parallel.

I want to thank another cousin and survivor of the holocaust, Phyllis Nissenbaum Linell. She is the granddaughter of Faige's sister Sarah. Her recollections of pre-World War II Skalat were pleasant and in sharp contrast to the holocaust.

My wife, Beverly Weinstock Lewitter, has exercised much patience in that she allowed me the time necessary to write the book. I thank her for her cooperation. The project could not have been done without her help and understanding. I want to thank my son David Nathan Lewitter, my son Ari Joseph Lewitter and his wife Deborah Melman Lewitter. I want to thank my stepson Dr. Alan Weinstock, his wife Joan Goldschmidt Weinstock, my stepdaughter Laurie Weinstock Hecht and her husband Louis Hecht. It is not easy for a writer to explain to his family that he is working on a book that concerns them but that most of the subject matter is unknown to them. To my grandchildren I pray that the book will help them understand the amazing sequence of events that took place before they were born.

Most of all, I want to thank the Almighty Himself, Who has blessed me, protected me and saved my life many times and has allowed me to write this book.

Dr. Sidney Rubin Lewitter
Long Branch, New Jersey
April, 1994

SKALAT, POLAND

# CHAPTER 1

★

*S*himon Halevy always felt triumphant as *Yom Kippur* drew to a close, knowing that he had once again fasted for twenty-six hours and lodged himself in the town synagogue for nearly as long. But this *Yom Kippur* was different. For the first time since he could remember, his mother hadn't come to the synagogue for *Neelah*. Shimon felt anxious.

He looked nervously at his father. Zvi Hersh, resplendent in his black *kapote* and huge prayer shawl, was swaying back and forth, immersed in his prayers. Shimon glanced at his younger brother Jacob. He also seemed oblivious to the situation.

Shimon hesitated for a moment, shifting on his long legs from foot to foot.

"Where is Mamme?" Shimon finally whispered to his father.

"Mamme felt faint," Zvi Hersh answered abruptly. "She went home to lie down." He cast a quick look at the women's balcony, shook his head apprehensively and returned to his *davening*.

Shimon felt a sudden qualm of dread. If his mother was sick enough to miss *Neelah*, her situation must certainly be serious. What is Tatte still doing in *shul* at a time like this? Shimon thought indignantly. He was tempted to say something, but fearful about being disrespectful towards his father, he kept quiet.

*Neelah* seemed to go on for hours before the *shofar* sounded the end of the long day. Disregarding well-meaning inquiries from friends and relatives, Shimon left his father outside the *shul* and hurried home at a trot, raising dust in the dirt street. Jacob kept pace behind him. When they reached the familiar cobblestones on the street near their home, they met their married sister Lortza at the door.

"Mamme is gone," she greeted them in a tear-choked whisper.

"That is impossible!" Shimon stammered, grasping the edge of the door to steady himself.

"Mamme is dead! Didn't you hear!" This time it was Rivka Reizah, his oldest sister, who shrieked the words at him. "She died just a few minutes ago."

Zvi Hersh crossed the wooden entryway into the house just as Rivka Reizah finished speaking. His large face was already red from his quickened return. He looked over his four children as he assessed the situation.

"Jacob, run back to the *shul* and tell the men of the *chevrah kadisha* that they will bury Mamme tonight," he ordered in a controlled voice. "Girls, get out all the candles in the house so we can light them around Mamme. Go to our neighbors for more candles if you need them."

By now, everyone was crying except Zvi Hersh, who continued to give instructions to his bewildered children. Finally, he motioned to Shimon to follow him into his deceased wife's room.

Shimon followed his father hesitantly. He had never seen a dead body before. The sight that greeted him brought forth a mingling of pain and morbid curiosity. Neshe Halevy was lying in her bed, still dressed in her holiday clothes. She was wearing her *sheitel*, which was the only indication that something was wrong—it was slightly askew atop her head. She must have died peacefully, Shimon thought. Her face was overrun by a compliant sorrow. She had died the way she had lived, with questions but without rebellion.

Zvi Hersh went to her side and closed her eyes. He was finally weeping, and Shimon realized that it was the first time he had ever seen his father cry. Shimon stood and watched the tears trickle into his father's thick black beard until he realized he was being watched by his son. Zvi Hersh quickly wiped his eyes and gestured to Shimon to help him lower Neshe Halevy to the floor.

Just then, four women from the *chevrah kadisha* burst into the room. They were carrying a big washing basin and shrouds. Almost at their heels, Rivka Reizah and Lortza rushed in with the candles that Zvi Hersh had requested. One of the women took them and ordered the family out of the room.

Neshe Halevy was buried that evening. Most of the Jewish community of Skalat joined the family in the short procession to the cemetery, many of them holding candles. Zvi Hersh bore himself with his customary dignity. At fifty-two, he was a huge, powerful man with a large round face and a full, well-groomed beard. Dominating his face were two piercing brown eyes that always divulged his mood long before he communicated it.

As Shimon and his father waited to begin the march to the cemetery, Shimon detected the pain in his father's eyes, now sunk deep into his face and surrounded by dark circles. Despite his earlier attempt at bravado, Shimon knew that his father was a crushed man. Mamme's death had been quick and unexpected, but he instinctively sensed that it wouldn't take long for his father to recover.

Shimon didn't feel the same about himself. At twenty-one, he contemplated that he was luckier than his eleven-year-old brother Jacob. Yet Shimon felt that he was the one who would miss his mother the most. He had been her eldest son after five daughters, and Neshe had been intensely proud of her boy, now grown into a tall, strong, and yet mild man. His gentle nature had endeared him to his mother, and the two had formed a loving and devoted relationship. The bond they shared far surpassed anything Shimon had with his father or, for that matter, Neshe had with her other children.

Though Jacob was not as close with his mother, her loss was as painful to him as it was to Shimon because of his age. And in the emotional hierarchy that governed turn-of-the-century Skalat, the right to cry among family members was accorded only to the women and younger children. Jacob, deemed too old for this license, suffered all the more as a result.

Three months after the death of his wife, Zvi Hersh married a woman who had never been married before and moved her and her elderly mother into the house. At thirty-seven, Zipporah Goodman was a small woman with careworn eyes and reddish hair. She had devoted her life to taking care of her parents. Her father had recently died, and Zipporah was left alone with her mother. Life was hard, money was scarce, and she welcomed the idea of marrying Zvi Hersh, who was considered affluent by Skalat standards.

Her first day in the house, she confronted Shimon and Jacob. "You've lost your mother, and you'll never have another," she informed them. "I am going to have enough to do with my own mother and my new husband."

"I don't want a new mother," responded Jacob.

"And you shouldn't need one any more than your older sisters do," Zipporah countered, unpacking her mother's few possessions. She turned to Shimon. "Shimon, you're twenty-one years old. Why haven't you married Faige Shapiro yet? She's a good girl from a good family. There's no reason to have such a long engagement."

Jacob jumped at his new stepmother. "Don't you dare tell my brother what to do! If you're not our mother, don't try to act like her!"

Zipporah reveled for a moment in the spiteful contentment that comes to people when their worst expectations about others have been confirmed. "My friends have told me you'd be a problem. You'll respect me as your father's wife, or I'll have your father talk with you."

Zvi Hersh's household changed dramatically after that. Save for the patriarch himself, none of its participants—Zipporah, her mother, Jacob and Shimon—felt in any way tied to this reconstituted unit. The death of Neshe Halevy signified the death of the Halevy family as Shimon and Jacob had known it. Their new life was to be full of change.

# CHAPTER 2

★

*A* couple of months after his father's remarriage, an opportunity presented itself to Shimon offering a new life away from the dismal family situation at home. But his father did not approve of it.

"Forget the letter, Shimon," Zvi Hersh told his son. "I intend to hire a substitute for you. I can easily arrange it. There is no reason for you to go into the army. This is not in the Russian part of Poland."

Shimon looked from his father down to the letter of conscription in his hand. He knew his father could arrange to have someone take his place in the Austrian army. Zvi Hersh was a man of influence in Skalat. He served on the local council that ran the city, and his stamp store often headquartered important activities for both the Jewish and the Gentile communities.

But Shimon didn't put the letter down. He wasn't going to give up so easily. Despite what he knew about the army and what little effort it would take to avoid conscription, he wanted to serve. The changing times of early-century Europe, missionized by the French revolution, had swept Shimon up in the belief that the world was surely improving. He felt privileged to live under the rule of enlightened Austria, a nation far more benign to the Jewish people than Germany or Russia, and he wanted to serve the Emperor Franz Joseph. Besides, he had been assured that he would be placed in charge of a horse-drawn cannon, and to a twenty-one-year-old Jew from Skalat, that prospect was exciting.

"Tatte knows," he ventured to reply, "that Austria is not Russia. The situation with Jewish boys in the Russian army is horrible, but I consider it an honor to serve the Kaiser."

"And how do you plan to live like a Jew in the army?" Zvi Hersh asked.

"That won't be a problem. I won't eat anything *treif*, and you know I like fruits and vegetables. I heard that I'll be stationed close to home, so I'll always be able to get food. I'll take my *tefillin* with me, and I'll make sure to *daven* every day. You don't have to worry about me."

Shimon was determined, and Zvi Hersh detected the resolve in his voice. For once, he let his son have his way. "Shimon, I think that you're a fool, but I'll let you go. I'll tell the Shapiro family that you'll marry Faige after you are finished with the army service, one year from now."

Zvi Hersh raised his huge frame and started to leave the room. Shimon was surprised at how easily his father had given in. He looked at his father as he was leaving and thought he saw a hint of admiration steal across his face. Typical, he thought. Nobody wins with Tatte unless he wants him to.

Shimon remained in the room after his father left, rereading the conscription notice and imagining what life in the army was going to be like. Suddenly, the door to the house banged open, and Jacob came charging in.

"Come quick!" he panted. "Rivka Reizah needs you at the inn. Kowalsky is on another one of his rampages!"

Shimon dropped his letter on the table and rushed after Jacob to his sister's inn. It wasn't the first time Rivka Reizah had called Shimon to curb a rowdy customer in the inn. At six foot five, Shimon cut an imposing figure. But Jan Kowalsky happened to be one of the more violent patrons. This time, when Shimon and Jacob reached the inn, they found the peasant in a terrifying, drunken stupor.

"I want my money, I want my money," he was shrieking.

For the fourth time, Rivka Reizah began to tell him that there was nothing coming to him. He had already spent all the money he had come in with. The sight of Shimon in the inn infuriated Kowalsky.

"Do you think you can scare me by calling in your big brother?" he shouted at Rivka Reizah. "He doesn't scare me. No Jew does. I would do the right thing if I killed you now."

With that murderous pronouncement, all the customers fled, leaving only the three Halevys to mollify the raging drunkard.

"There is no need for such screaming and shouting," Shimon said calmly, walking towards Kowalsky. "You have no money left, that's it. Leave now, and there won't be any problems."

Shimon stopped within a few steps of Kowalsky, and the two sized each other up. Then Shimon dropped his hands, indicating to Kowalsky that he was ready to walk out of the tavern with him, but Kowalsky wound his hands into fists and struck Shimon fully on the jaw. Shimon's head fell back, and blood began to spurt from his mouth.

Rivka Reizah screamed, and Jacob edged towards Kowalsky holding a chair. Even then, Shimon sought to pacify the man and insisted they leave the inn. But Kowalsky would not be reconciled. His fists still raised, he danced about, looking for an opportunity to strike Shimon again. He never found it. Shimon finally hoisted his hands up and swung a powerhouse blow to Kowalsky's face, buckling Kowalsky's knees and snapping him to the floor.

"Nobody cheats you here," Shimon said to Kowalsky in a slow and deliberate voice. "You spend your money as you see fit. When it's gone, that's it. Terrorizing us will not work. Now Jan, I'm urging you to get up, and the two of us will walk out together."

Shimon and Kowalsky both knew that a crowd had gathered outside the inn, and Shimon did not want to inflict the *coup de grace* on his antagonist by deporting him before the milling witnesses. For once, Kowalsky complied. But as he withdrew from the inn, Jacob heard him mumble, "I'll get you for this, if it takes a lifetime."

# CHAPTER 3

★

*S*himon joined the Austrian cavalry in December, 1907, and was commissioned to tend a horse-drawn cannon, as promised. The horse was magnificent, and Shimon called him Grosse Ferd, or big horse, in Yiddish. Shimon was charged with maintaining this equine beauty, grooming it as if it were the prize of the emperor's own stable.

Rider and horse soon acquired a mutual respect. Even with little riding experience, Shimon had no trouble enforcing his benevolent control over Grosse Ferd. He loved to lead and ride the horse. Shimon felt useful and important when he was mounted atop Grosse Ferd. While riding him, he tasted a feeling of power and freedom that far exceeded anything he had experienced in Skalat.

Though the camp was on the outskirts of Skalat, and the trip home was easily negotiated, Shimon did not often return there. Not seeing his father, even when that prospect regularly held itself out to him, certified his nascent freedom. Shimon began to wonder if his ardor for the military was a means of devotion to the Emperor or a pretext to distance himself from his family.

Shimon also discouraged his father from sending kosher meat to him in the camp. He knew that his fellow soldiers would be envious of the food, and he was afraid of being robbed or beaten by anyone who wanted the provisions badly enough. Besides, he could easily obtain food in any of the neighboring cities. He would buy a large salami or bologna, layer it on black bread and crown the sandwich with whatever vegetables he could get, usually onions. Beer or *schnapps* nicely rounded out his major daily meal.

One April afternoon, a surprised Shimon eyed Jacob struggling up the hill to where he was eating one of his salami sandwiches. "Well, look who's here! Welcome to my house. Do you want any salami and bread?"

Jacob shook his head. "I hope I'm not intruding, but I had to get away," he began. "You can go stir crazy lingering in the house, and there is nothing to do in the streets, either."

"Aren't you supposed to be in school?" Shimon asked him.

"I'm too old for school. Even the teachers can't decide what class I'm in."

"Have you talked to Tatte about it?"

"Tatte doesn't even know I exist. I never talk to him."

Shimon didn't reply. He knew that if he had remained at home, his father probably wouldn't have paid him much attention either. Luckily, he was in the army. He felt sorry for his younger brother. With an indifferent father and a hostile stepmother, what options did eleven-year-old Jacob have?

Jacob sensed his brother's empathy. With a swift glance around the top of the hill, Jacob inched closer to Shimon and spoke in a low voice.

"I have a plan," he said, pausing for emphasis. "I'm going to go to America." He leaned back to gauge Shimon's reaction.

"America?" Shimon exclaimed. "You're only eleven years old!"

"Well, I'm not going to leave immediately. I have it all planned out. I'll go to Mamme's sister, Tante Frieda. It's been almost five years since she left for America. You remember how you used to take me to her house. She was always nice to us. I heard that she and her children own a grocery store in Jersey City, that's near New York City. I'm sure that if I go to Tante Frieda, she'll help me get settled. I have my mind made up, Shimon. There's nothing for me to do in Skalat."

"Look Jacob, I'm not telling you that you shouldn't go," Shimon explained, finding himself siding with his brother. "You should know, though, that it's not going to be easy. You'll need at least two hundred dollars in American money to get there. You can't expect Tatte to give you that money so that you can leave him. And before you do anything, you should write to Tante Frieda so that she can help you with any papers you may need. And what about your *bar-mitzvah*? You can't leave without having your *bar-mitzvah* here."

"Of course, I will wait, Shimon," said Jacob. "You know that. It will probably take me the year and a half to work out my plans anyhow."

Shimon looked at his brother in admiration. For an eleven-year-old boy, Jacob was impressively ambitious and independent. Seeing how badly he wanted it, Shimon sensed that Jacob would make it safely to America and probably succeed there as well.

"You know, Jacob, I think you've got yourself a great plan. And if there is anything . . ." Shimon stopped in mid-sentence. He thought he heard something in the distance. Gradually, the noise became more distinct.

Shimon and Jacob looked down the hill to see a band of vague, enlarging figures and heard the belligerent shouts of laughing men. As the group drew closer to the foot of the hill, they recognized Kowalsky, surrounded by a dozen thugs.

Shimon huddled close to Jacob and put his finger over his mouth. "Lie down and keep quiet," he whispered. "This is meant for me. I can't let them know that you are here. You have to get help. Crawl on your stomach to that end of the hill opposite the men. Don't get up until you're all the way down and can't be seen. Then get up and run as fast as you can. Go to Sarah Elfenbein's tavern and try to get Rosenkranz."

Shimon inspected the fierce group of men at the foot of the hill. Captain Rosenkranz, a local Austrian officer whose peacemaking talents were often requisitioned by tavern owners, might be his only chance. Faige Shapiro's sister, Sarah Elfenbein, owned an inn where Rosenkranz often spent time. Shimon hoped to Heaven that he would be there now.

As Jacob crawled to the other end of the hill, Shimon stood up and drew his sword. "You had better be careful, Kowalsky," he shouted. "One of us could really get hurt this time."

"You're right, Shimon," Kowalsky called back. "One of us will get hurt this time, and it's not going to be me. You can come down the hill by yourself and pray for a miracle on the way, or we will come up and get you."

Kowalsky stood with his legs apart and a bottle of whiskey protruding from his hand. For a moment, Shimon considered mounting Grosse Ferd and charging the mob with his sword. He was sure he could get most of them before they would get him. But he rejected the idea as suicidal and decided he would be a more elusive target on foot.

Shimon secured his horse to a tree and started down the hill, sword poised. He slowly treaded down the hill with desperate deliberation, hoarding the minutes he needed to give Rosenkranz a chance to reach him.

Halfway down the hill, Shimon stopped altogether. He

thought of one last ploy to dissuade Kowalsky. "You're making a mistake, Jan," he warned. "If you kill me, you're not just killing a Skalat Jew. I am a member of the Emperor's army. Somebody will claim that you started an insurrection by killing a soldier of the Austrian government."

To Shimon's amazement, Kowalsky seemed to consider the logic in Shimon's argument. He shifted from one foot to the other and looked back at his gang.

"Look fellows," he reasoned, "he may be right. There might be some commotion in the army if they find out that we did him in. We don't have to kill him, let's just teach him a lesson he'll never forget."

"All right," Kowalsky said, turning back to Shimon, "we'll spare you this time. Come down, but drop your sword first and let it roll down the hill. If you don't, we will come up to get you."

Shimon dropped his sword on the grass and kicked it with his foot, gently enough to be able to rearm himself on the way down.

Kowalsky was getting impatient. "I'm tired of waiting," he shouted. "Let's go get him!"

As the men rushed up the hill, Shimon raced towards his sword. Before he could grab the blade, the men were upon him. Whirling around, Shimon picked up the man nearest to him and threw him at another. Then he grabbed the unclaimed sword and struck out at the closest man. It happened to be Kowalsky, who careened to the ground, badly lacerated and screaming.

It was a premature victory. The other men fell over Shimon, knocking his sword away and beating him with their fists and feet. One of the men grabbed Shimon's sword and held it above Shimon. He asked the wounded Kowalsky if he should finish him off.

All of a sudden, seemingly from nowhere, a shot was fired into the air. "You had better not or I will kill you!"

Shimon and the gang of thugs looked up to see Rosenkranz dismounting his horse. Behind Rosenkranz, they saw a company of soldiers approaching.

"Put Shimon in the wagon," Rosenkranz ordered the soldiers, "and arrest the others. I charge them with assaulting one of the Kaiser's loyal soldiers."

# CHAPTER 4

★

*S*himon was saved that day on the hill. His recovery, however, took many weeks and was won only by the determined and dedicated care of Faige and Rivka Reizah, at whose home he convalesced.

Faige travelled almost every day to see Shimon. She lived with her mother a mile outside of Skalat on a small farm that had been bought for her father, Rabbi Kalman Yosef Shapiro, by the local townspeople. Rabbi Shapiro was a pious and learned man who had served as the unofficial rabbi for the Jews of his area for many years. He had refused an official appointment, because he felt that the people were too poor to support a rabbi.

The farm enabled the Shapiros to grow some vegetables for the family's consumption and for general sale. Still, they were very poor. Rabbi Shapiro died in his fifties when Faige was only eighteen. Her sister Sarah and brother Eliyahu were already married, and Faige lived with her mother alone on the farm for three years following her father's death.

While Shimon was convalescing, he and Faige were able to spend more time with each other than they had since they had gotten engaged. Like most of the marriages in Skalat, Shimon's and Faige's future marriage was arranged by their parents, and the two had little opportunity to get to know one another before Shimon's near-disaster with Kowalsky.

Now Shimon thought a lot about what his future with Faige would be like. Young couples in Skalat did not have it easy. The only available way for most couples to earn a living was by doing business. Shimon knew his shortcomings. His diffident nature would never accommodate the driving business ethic. At the same time, Shimon knew he was not prepared to earn a livelihood in any other way. He envied his father's ability to manage a successful stamp and tobacco store and serve as an important political figure in Skalat at the same time. Instinctively, he felt he would not be able to duplicate his father's successes. He knew he would try though, because he would never want to let Faige down.

Shimon's recovery prompted a new assessment of his situation. During a visit once by Sarah Elfenbein and Captain Rosenkranz, the conversation turned to Shimon's position in the army.

"I don't think it's a good idea for you to go back to the army," Sarah began. "There are people there who wish that Kowalsky had been able to finish you off. If you go back, you'll be putting yourself in a dangerous position."

"I have to go back," Shimon insisted, "or it will look like I'm running away."

"I agree," Sarah replied, "you certainly don't want to look like a coward. So Captain Rosenkranz and I have a plan. You're not completely recovered yet, and *Pesach* is only two weeks away. You're expected to have a leave for the holidays anyhow. You could go back to the army after *Pesach* for around six weeks, and Rosenkranz will keep you safe during that short time. That should give your father enough time to buy your replacement. This way, it won't look as if you're leaving the army because of the attack."

"You ought to do what Sarah says," Rosenkranz advised. "The feud is not just between you and Kowalsky any more. A dozen men feel that you've beaten them, and in a sense you have, just by living through the attack. I'm sure all of them are eager to finish off the job they started. Besides, the Jewish community regards you as a hero now. You might not be so lucky the next time around, and you wouldn't want to disappoint them."

"I have an even better reason for you to leave the army," Faige suggested eagerly. "We can move our wedding up from the end of December to the end of June."

All four began to laugh.

"That's the best idea of all!" Shimon finally said. "I guess you're all right."

# CHAPTER 5

★

*S*himon returned to camp after *Pesach* and received anew his uniform, horse, cannon and the sword that had saved his life. But he was unable to resume the army life he had been used to. The soldiers seemed to eye him warily now, and while he could not point to any case of outright rudeness, he encountered even less friendliness than before.

"Of course, things are different," said Igmore, a fellow soldier Shimon had previously befriended. "Before they only hated you; now they're afraid of you, too."

Shimon was dismayed. "That doesn't make sense. For the Jew, anti-semitism is a no-win situation. I'm hated if I am weak, and I'm hated if I am strong. If I am poor, the gentile says that I deserve to be poor. If I am rich, I became so by being dishonest. It's impossible to exist, let alone win anything."

"That's exactly it, Shimon," Igmore continued. "You're not supposed to win anything. It strikes me that you came into the army in the first place because you wanted to see what the world outside of Skalat looks like. Well, this is what it looks like. By the way, I noticed that you are followed quite closely by two men. They almost seem like bodyguards. Is that intentional?" Without waiting for Shimon's answer, Igmore supplied it himself. "Probably Rosenkranz's men, ordered to protect you."

Shimon was astounded by his friend's grasp of the situation.

"Good idea," Igmore added.

Six weeks later, Shimon was honorably discharged from the army with a citation for meritorious duty of which he was never proud. He left the army camp bereft of his prize attachments—Grosse Ferd, the cannon, his uniform and his sword. Shimon had loved his military service but knew that the experiment had failed.

Zvi Hersh didn't show any outward signs of emotion at having Shimon back at home, but Shimon knew that the sight of his son in civilian clothes gladdened his father.

"This is my son," he told Shimon on his first night home. "This is the way I like to see him."

For the next few weeks, Shimon was busy preparing his future home. He had little time left, since the wedding date was set for *Rosh Chodesh Tammuz*, 1908. He also started to work in the grain store that his mother used to operate. He and Faige had plans to operate the shop after their wedding. The beginning weeks were not too successful, but Shimon was sure business would pick up after the wedding, when he could devote his full concentration to it.

The preparations and festivities were not just limited to the family, however. For the Jews in Skalat, every *simchah* was savored. Life was hard and drab, and a wedding or *bar-mitzvah* lifted the mood of the community above the bearable and unified it around a cause for joy.

The entire Jewish community of Skalat was invited to the

wedding, which would take place in the *shul* and on the streets in front of it. Since the building could not host so many people, the guests would stay for a while and then leave to accommodate others. They would bring food and liquor with them, continuously replenishing the feast with new provisions.

Zvi Hersh had obtained scores of chickens, and Zipporah distributed them to friends and relatives who would prepare them. A friend who accepted five chickens invariably tried to give back more than she had received, the additional chickens representing her gift. Faige's mother baked *kugels* and pastries and provided the fruits and vegetables, exotic additions to a Skalat wedding. Sarah Elfenbein delivered the *schnapps* and vodka.

On the Sunday before the wedding, Sarah visited her sister Faige. She found Faige in the bedroom, trying on her wedding dress and admiring herself in the mirror.

"You look beautiful, Faige," Sarah began. "I've noticed how happy you've been these past couple of weeks."

"Yes, I am happy," Faige answered confidently.

"And I hope you will be after you get married, too."

"What do you mean by that?" Faige was taken by surprise.

"Well, marriage is not easy in Skalat," Sarah said, rather dourly. "And I don't mean just for the women. The men don't have it much easier than we do, but it's the women who usually end up doing most of the work. In my case, I just can't trust my husband to run the tavern. It would collapse in a week if I left it to him. And it's like that for most of the couples I know."

Faige looked at her sister dubiously.

"Tell me," Sarah pressed on, "who stayed in our produce store most of the time, Mamme or Tatte?"

"But that was different," Faige corrected her sister. "Tatte was a rabbi."

"True," Sarah admitted, "but the problem remains the same

for many of the men. They are just not inclined to be shopkeepers. They were brought up learning Torah, and many of them don't consider business a noble enterprise or are capable of running one. Shimon strikes me as the type who wants to be liked, something that is very difficult for a storeowner, I'm afraid."

Faige didn't answer. She turned away from Sarah and began fingering the buttons on her dress. She didn't know about other couples, but she had suspected Shimon might not make the ideal storeowner. She was upset that her sister had confirmed her private suspicions, and she didn't want Sarah to know how she felt.

Suddenly, Sarah felt sorry for her. She walked over to Faige and hugged her. She thought she had been doing her sister a favor by cautioning her, but now she felt guilty at having brought all this up right before the wedding.

"I'm sorry, Faige. Maybe I was wrong about Shimon. He's a fine person, and I'm sure you'll be very happy with him. One thing is for sure—we are going to have one of the biggest and most exciting weddings that Skalat has ever seen."

Sarah was right. When the day of the wedding finally arrived, Shimon arrived in a new *kapote* and a new *shtreimel*, given to him by his father. Leah Shapiro gave her daughter her wedding dress, a cherished Shapiro family heirloom, along with the *sheitel* she would wear as a married woman.

Jacob delivered a present to Shimon from his future wife—a *tallis* chosen by his late father-in-law, Rabbi Kalman Yosef Shapiro, and given to Faige for her future husband.

Shimon fingered the *tallis* gently and called after Jacob as he left. "I don't know what jobs they have picked out for you during the wedding, but try to stay as close to me as possible."

"I promise," Jacob answered loyally.

As the Halevy procession approached the *shul*, hundreds of

people convened in front, opening a path for the family. When they saw Shimon, the crowd broke into song.

The *chupah* went smoothly, but Shimon noticed that Jacob practically dropped one of the poles he was hoisting for the *chupah* in his eagerness to get closer to Shimon.

The happiness was pervasive, and few could hold back tears of joy. The couple was so young. Shimon was loved and admired. He was a hero. Faige was a beautiful bride with an honored lineage. The new pair had already endeared itself to the town, and the effect was euphoric.

For the next six days, the singing and dancing continued during the *sheva berachos*. The last one of the *sheva berachos*, at the home of Eliyahu Shapiro, had a sobering effect on Faige and Shimon. They knew that the next day would be the first normal one of the rest of their lives. The store would open, and it would be a market day besides. But each felt that the celebrations they had just enjoyed would last them for a long time to come.

# CHAPTER 6

★

*S*himon's business problems began the very day he and Faige opened the grain store. Early in the morning, he rented a horse and wagon and left for the mill to purchase his grain supply.

The mill owner, Ivan Padonsky, had known Shimon as a boy, who for many years had accompanied his mother for purchases. He was sure he would have no problems dealing with the miller.

Shimon was shocked at how Padonsky received him. Not only did he not congratulate Shimon on his marriage, but he was downright rude.

"I suppose you will be coming regularly from now on for flour to sell in your mother's store," he began curtly. "Well, you should know in advance that I won't have much time to spend with you. When you do come, you'll need money, preferably foreign currency. I don't trust the Austrian mark any more. Also, the money will have to be in advance."

Shimon wasn't sure how to reply. "Sir," he ventured, "you surely recall that our relationship goes back a long time. Neither I nor my mother had ever been negligent in paying our bills. I see no reason why we shouldn't continue to do business together as we used to do for many years to come."

"Well, I do," Padonsky retorted. "You weren't a big man then. I don't know if I can or want to do business with a Jewish hero."

"That's unfair, Mr. Padonsky. I am not a hero nor do I want to be one. I simply responded to an unfair attack against me, as you or anybody else would have done. Why should that have any bearing on our business relationship?"

"You're naive, Shimon, terribly naive," Padonsky declaimed. "Look, I've spent enough time with you already. Take your merchandise, pay for it and leave. In the future, you would do better to come with Faige. Send her into the mill. I would rather deal with her than with you. While she's in the mill, you can stay with the horse and wagon, like you used to when your mother was alive."

Shimon let this last insult pass and hurried to complete his transaction. As he left, Shimon saw Padonsky and several others gesturing at him contemptuously. What a terrible hate they must feel toward me, he thought.

Shimon came home to Faige rattled and dispirited, but when he saw how eager and excited she was about their first day of business, he decided to delay telling her of the day's events for as long as possible.

A few days later, however, Shimon and Faige faced another crisis of a different sort.

"My sister Sarah was right," Faige confirmed to her husband, with little satisfaction. "Tell me, Shimon, how much did you charge Mrs. Schwartz for the five-pound bag of flour that you just gave her?"

Shimon raised his eyebrows at this unexpected question. "Nothing," he told his wife, inflecting the word to let Faige know that it was the only proper answer. "I charged her nothing."

"You charged her nothing?" Faige was incredulous. "I can't believe that—you charged her nothing? Why did you do that?"

"How can I charge her anything?" Shimon answered guilessly. "She's a widow struggling to raise four little children. The Torah tells us to look out for widows and orphans. I did just that. I couldn't charge her."

Faige tried to control her anger. "Tell me, Shimon, how about yesterday with Mrs. Katz? How much did you charge *her* for a five-pound bag of flour?"

"I took whatever money she had."

"And what was that?"

"About half the amount she should have paid," Shimon answered rather sheepishly. "I couldn't help it. Her husband is very sick, and they have six children. That was all the money she had. I couldn't deny her flour to feed her family, could I? Come on, Faige, what kind of a man do you think I am?"

"But, Shimon, don't you see what you are doing?" Faige pressed him. "Look at the pattern that is developing here. There are many poor Jews in Skalat. Once word gets out that they don't have to pay us for the flour they need, we'll always be the last ones to be paid. At that rate, how long do you think it will be before we can't pay Mr. Padonsky? We can't be in business this way. I know we have to give away a certain amount of charity, but it can't come out of our business like this. By the way, speaking of Mr. Padonsky, it's time to go back for some more flour."

"I'm afraid you'll have to come with me," he said apologetically and recounted his confrontation with Padonsky at the mill.

Faige sat down on the stool next to her and shook her head. "We're off to a difficult start, aren't we, Shimon? First, we have trouble getting the flour, and after we get it, you want to give it away."

"I'm sorry," Shimon said. He looked down at the floor and leaned against the wall with slumped shoulders. A long silence ensued.

Finally, Faige got up from the stool and crossed the room to Shimon. "Let's not worry too much. I'm sure we'll come up with some way to deal with Padonsky. But before we go, we're going to have to develop some rules of charity that will let us stay in business."

Shimon was moved by his wife's equanimity. "God bless you, Faige. Perhaps some day I'll be truly worthy of you."

Before they could continue further, they were distracted by shouts coming through the open window. Faige quickly went to the window and looked out, but she could see nothing. The clamor got louder.

"It almost sounds like a pogrom," she said nervously.

Shimon cautiously opened the side door and stepped out. After a couple of moments, he motioned for Faige to come. "It's not a pogrom, but something is definitely going on."

The two of them carefully walked to the edge of the street and tried to discern from which direction the noise was coming.

"Let's head that way," Shimon said and turned right with Faige in tow.

They passed screaming people running in every direction, and as they approached the center of the commotion they realized they were headed right for Sarah Elfenbein's tavern. When they got there, Faige gave out a shriek of alarm and ran towards the door. A soldier blocking the entrance recognized Faige and Shimon and moved aside to allow them in.

The tavern inside was in a shambles. Tables and chairs were overturned, and shards of broken whiskey bottles impaled the furniture. There was a strong stench of liquor seeping through the floors.

Shimon and Faige surveyed the scene in shock. Then suddenly, Faige screamed and pointed to the front of the room near the bar. There, sprawled across the length of the bar, was Jan Kowalsky with a huge knife sprouting from his chest.

The door to the bar opened just then, and a bleeding Captain Rosenkranz clambered out, followed by Sarah Elfenbein. He saw Shimon and called him over. "Come here, Shimon. You too, Faige. I want you both to see your archenemy. If I hadn't killed him, I'm sure that, sooner or later, you would have had to do it."

"What happened?" Faige asked incredulously.

"You tell them, Sarah," Rosenkranz said, sitting down on one of the only chairs still standing, "but give me a drink first."

He pulled a handkerchief from his pocket and pressed it against a bleeding wound on his forehead. Sarah scavenged an intact bottle, wiped it on her dress and gave it to Rosenkranz. Turning to Shimon and Faige, she began to recount what had happened.

"As you both probably know, Kowalsky has been coming to my tavern ever since his fight with you at Rivka Reizah's. I didn't care. I have all sorts of people coming to my place. In this business, you don't choose your customers.

"Kowalsky was always a rough man, but he's been almost brutal after he lost his arm fighting you, Shimon. If it wasn't for Captain Rosenkranz's protection, I have no doubt that he would have killed you long ago. Your wedding drove him over the edge. He couldn't take seeing how the whole community regarded you as a hero."

"But what happened here? How did he get killed?" Shimon was getting impatient with Sarah's commentary.

"I'm getting to that," Sarah said. "He came here early today in a terrible mood. It took him only a half hour to get drunk. Captain Rosenkranz came in around a half hour later, and Kowalsky really went wild. He started cursing Rosenkranz and calling him a traitor and a Jew-lover. He grabbed a bottle of whiskey and broke it over Captain Rosenkranz's head. Rosenkranz started to defend himself. The two got in a fight, and the other customers here took sides. But when Rosenkranz saw Kowalsky reach for a gun in his coat pocket, he pulled out his knife and killed him."

"That's the way it happened," corroborated Rosenkranz. He put down the half-finished whiskey bottle he was drinking and looked at the front door. The police hadn't come yet.

"Shimon, help me move his body," Rosenkranz instructed, getting up. "We'll take it to the police if they don't show up soon. Faige, help Sarah clean up the place. She still has to make a living."

He laughed wryly at his little joke, and Sarah smiled. But Shimon and Faige were grim. Captain Rosenkranz's paid protection had certainly paid off, but they were not rejoicing at the death of their antagonist. They couldn't believe it had come to this.

Things settled down for a time after Kowalsky's death. No one mentioned the attacker's name or even recalled his life or spectacular death. Shimon and Faige were relieved they no longer had to worry about Kowalsky, but they were now confronted with another antagonist.

A few days later Faige approached Shimon. "Shimon, I hate to bring up the subject, but we have to go back to Padonsky for more flour."

"I know," Shimon agreed, "but I'm afraid you'll have to go with me. I know he'll sell us the flour. If he didn't want to sell, he would have said so. He is not a bashful man. I'll tell you this though, if he so much as lays a hand on you, I'll kill him."

"Don't worry," Faige said.

But Faige was worried. The situation was perilous. They needed flour to stay in business, and Padonsky was their most efficient source. In fact, he was probably their only source. For the past few days, Faige had been plotting a way to win Padonsky over to their side. She had made calculations on her own but didn't disclose them to Shimon. She didn't want to disappoint him if her plan failed.

On the day she and Shimon planned to go to Padonsky, Faige silently practiced what she would say over and over. She decided what tone she would adopt. She would be friendly, yet businesslike.

Faige was quiet on the way to the flour mill. Shimon knew she was nervous, and he felt guilty.

"Good luck, Faige," he said as he dropped her off in front of the mill. "If you need me for any reason, just call out my name."

Faige descended the carriage and walked up the few steps into the mill. She found Mr. Padonsky at the counter and drew in a deep breath before she greeted him.

"Hello, Mr. Padonsky, I am Faige Halevy. I hope that you remember me; we've met once or twice."

Padonsky looked at her, a little disconcerted by Faige's forthrightness. "Well, if it isn't the new bride. Where is your hero husband?" he asked sarcastically.

"He's out in the front with the horse. I thought we could do the talking," Faige answered, skirting the affront. "You know that Shimon and I will be operating the grain store in Skalat, and there are a number of things I thought I would like to discuss."

"Such as?" Padonsky asked curiously.

"Such as Mr. Schultz," Faige replied.

"What about him?" Padonsky looked surprised.

Faige was pleased at how she had managed to capture Padonsky's interest so quickly. She continued speaking in a confident tone. "We both know Mr. Schultz is the other flour dealer in Skalat. He does a much bigger business than Shimon and I can expect to do. I have a plan that would benefit us, enable you to make a bigger profit and, in the long run, even help Mr. Schultz."

Padonsky raised his eyebrows. Now he was very interested. "What kind of plan do you have?"

"The idea is to undersell Mr. Schultz." Here Faige paused and waited a moment to see Padonsky's reaction. He said nothing, and she continued. "Mr. Schultz sells all his flour one day a week—on Tuesday, the market day. Plus, he only sells to farmers. We're open six days a week, and we sell to everybody, including farmers.

"If you gave us a discount on the flour, we would be able to undersell Mr. Schultz. You would only be giving us a short-term advantage, however. It wouldn't take long for Schultz to realize what we would be doing. He would be forced to cut his own prices. He might even stay open another day or two a week in order to sell more. People in Skalat do not use as much flour as they would like because it's expensive. If prices came down, we would both sell more. You would benefit with a higher volume, and Mr. Schultz would wake up to the market potential in Skalat, in addition to selling to farmers."

Padonsky looked at Faige suspiciously. "And what about you?"

"We couldn't lose. Even if Mr. Schultz gets more of the business, we'd still have enough, because there will be so much more business to share. People will start coming to Skalat for flour from all over. If we see that too many of our customers are buying from Mr. Schultz, we can take our low-priced flour to Lemberg or even Tarnapol one or two days a week and sell right off the wagon. We can even go to some Russian towns that are nearby and sell flour to peasants. The future would be up to us, you and me. We would decide how big we wanted to get."

Faige was exhausted. She had given all of her strength, courage and optimism to her presentation. Now she stood back, looked at Padonsky and awaited his assessment.

Mr. Padonsky didn't react for some time. Faige could tell he was silently considering her plan. Then suddenly, his face broke out into a huge smile. "Faige, it's beautiful, it's absolutely beautiful. What a businesswoman you are!"

Faige breathed a sigh of relief.

"Call in Shimon," Padonsky said to Faige. "We'll have a drink and celebrate our new partnership."

Shimon couldn't contain himself on the trip home. "I can't get over it. What did you say to him? When we came to the mill the problem was whether Padonsky would sell us flour at all. Not only were we able to buy the flour, but we left with a full wagon at a reduced rate, and he considers us his partners. What happened?"

"I simply spoke business sense, and he bought it. I just hope everything works out the way I said it would."

# CHAPTER 7

★

*F*aige's business scheme turned out to be a success, and the grain store was turning in a nice profit. But soon Shimon and Faige encountered what turned out to be another rather dangerous setback in their business. A week after *Sukkos*, Skalat was the scene of a devastating pogrom. A hundred Cossacks on horseback raged into the town in the early morning, and luckily so, since most of the residents were in their homes at that hour. The horsemen used their swords at whim to maim and murder hapless early risers and destroy anything in their path. All the while, the Austrian army and police hid from the population it had sworn to protect.

As soon as it became obvious to Shimon that he was witnessing the early stages of a major raid, he took steps to protect Faige. "Faige, you stay under the bed until I give the all-clear signal. I'll see if there is anything that I can do to keep them from destroying everything that we have. Please—stay out of sight."

"Shimon, it's more important that you take care of yourself," Faige implored and gathered herself under the bed. "I don't care what they take, don't fight them or they'll kill you."

Shimon ignored her plea and headed for the grain store to secure the locks on the door. A rider on a huge horse saw Shimon closing the store door.

"What do you have in there, Jew?" he demanded.

"Flour," answered Shimon.

"Flour?" the Cossack replied. "Good. We need flour. How much do you have?"

"We just received a load yesterday; the store is full of flour."

"Did you hear that, men? This Jew has a store full of flour. Get a wagon over here, and let's relieve him of it."

Half a dozen Cossacks rode towards the store and started to dismount. But the first Cossack remained where he was, looking down at Shimon. This is it, Shimon thought. There was no place to run. The Cossack's horse made Grosse Ferd look like a pony, and when topped by its fearsome mount, seemed to reach ten feet in the air. The Cossack's long sword was unsheathed. Fighting was impossible.

"Jew, I have decided to pay you for the flour," the Cossack jeered at him.

"You will?" answered Shimon incredulously.

"Yes, I am going to let you live."

Shortly afterward, the Cossacks stormed out of Skalat as swiftly as they had arrived, having killed about fifty people, wounded two hundred more and looted much of the town. Shimon and Faige had survived their first pogrom.

They went to survey the wreckage in their store that evening. "Shimon, if they stole our flour, why did they have to break our shelves?"

"Power, Faige, power. How else are we to know that they are the bosses?" Shimon said sardonically. "What I really don't understand is why the Cossack didn't kill me."

"Because God wanted you to live," his wife answered.

A second pogrom took place almost six months to the day later. Carried out a week after *Pesach*, it far surpassed the first rampage in violence. Once again, Shimon hid Faige under her bed, but he did not go out to meet the invaders this time, hiding instead in a false ceiling.

From the sounds in the store, Shimon and Faige knew that the looters were again carrying off bags of flour. They waited until they thought they heard the last of the Cossacks smashing shelves and carting off the bags. Then Faige inched her way to the front of the bed and tried to peek out from under the blanket that hid her. Just then, she heard the door to the house crash open, and she quickly edged back towards the wall.

A Cossack ran into the bedroom and demanded to know if anyone was there. Greeted by silence, he gripped his sword and began to splinter the room. Shimon was distraught but let the Cossack have his way, until the intruder swung his sword under the bed where Faige cowered. He shoved the false ceiling out of the way and jumped on the back of the Cossack. The two of them fell to the floor, and the Cossack's sword dropped from his hand. Shimon seized the opportunity. He grabbed his enemy's throat and squeezed it as hard as he could. When he was sure that he had killed him, Shimon whispered to Faige to come out.

Faige squeezed her way out of the bed and stood next to Shimon. When she saw the dead Cossack, she gave out a stifled shriek of horror. The two of them stood shuddering in front of the body, not knowing what to do. After a few silent moments, Shimon shoved the body under the bed, while Faige hoisted herself up and hid in the false ceiling. Then he crawled under the bed alongside of the body.

After ten long minutes, the Cossacks began to leave town.

His experience with the first raid had taught Shimon that the leaving of the Cossacks was as precipitous as their entry. Shimon held his breath. Would anyone come looking for the missing Cossack? Shimon waited an hour longer and then emerged from under the bed. He helped Faige down from the ceiling. A moment later, Faige joined him, both of them surveying the scene around them.

"What should we do with the body?" she asked.

"I think we should drop it near the City Hall," Shimon answered, "but nobody must know of this, not even our own people. He has to appear as a casualty of the raid. I don't want to have him in our house until night, and besides, people would think it more natural if it was discovered right after the raid. I think we should put the body into the wagon, cover it with rags and drop it near the City Hall when no one is looking."

Faige helped Shimon hoist the Cossack's body into the wagon and cover him with rags. Then a nervous Shimon drove off. The plan worked perfectly. No one in Skalat ever knew who had killed one of the invading Cossacks.

All through that spring, Shimon and Faige were busy repairing their store from the damage the Cossacks had wrought and building up business. In the meantime, Shimon's brother Jacob was busy building his own plans for the future.

Ever since Jacob's confidential talk with Shimon about America, Jacob could not put the idea to rest. He talked to Shimon about it numerous times but never put any ideas into motion. He just knew that he had to go. His situation at home, especially with Zipporah, was deteriorating, and his relationship with his father was becoming more and more estranged. There were times when weeks would go by and the two would have nothing to say to one another. He almost never went to school and could find nothing with which to occupy himself.

Some time before *Rosh Hashanah*, Jacob's situation was brought to his father's attention. His sister, Pesya had a son, and Jacob's teacher from school had been invited to the *bris*. When the teacher went to congratulate Zvi Hersh on his new grandson, he complained to him about Jacob's erratic attendance in *cheder* and advised that Jacob be sent to a full-time *yeshivah* immediately following his *bar-mitzvah*. Zvi Hersh blew up at his son when he heard this.

"Leave him alone," Shimon intervened. "The boy is going through many hard adjustments."

"Things don't have to be that hard for him," Zvi Hersh retorted. "Jacob just makes everything complicated."

"It's not easy for Jacob," Shimon tried to explain. "His life drastically changed after Mamme died. He is lonely and angry, and he doesn't see a future for himself in Skalat. He doesn't have anyone to turn to. Jacob loves you, but he is afraid of you. He feels that you don't give him enough attention."

Zvi Hersh did not answer but instead busied himself with the guests at the *bris*. Shimon thought that perhaps his father knew that he was right and was reluctant to admit any fault of his own regarding Jacob.

A few weeks later, Jacob visited Shimon and Faige with his America-bound cousin, Shmuel Gross, Tante Frieda's son. The two cousins had been in close contact after Jacob had told Shmuel about his intention to go to America. He had asked Shmuel to find out whether his mother would help him out.

Shmuel related what his mother had recently written to him regarding Jacob's request. "My mother says that she can't afford to send him a shipscard for passage, but she is perfectly willing to sign all of the papers that guarantee the United States government that Jacob will come to us and not become a ward of the state. The rest is up to Jacob. He has to raise the money he needs to travel to America. Once he gets there, we'll help him find work and get him started."

Shimon looked at Faige. "Maybe we could try to raise some of the money for Jacob."

Jacob squelched the idea. "I wouldn't accept it, Shimon. You will be the one who will have to answer to Tatte after I'm gone, and I want you to be able to say that you had nothing to do with my going to America. I don't want him to think of you as an accomplice. Besides, I won't be going until after my *bar-mitzvah*, so I have time to come up with some ideas."

The time passed quickly. Jacob's *bar-mitzvah* ceremony was held on the *Shabbos* following *Yom Kippur*. Shimon could tell from his brother's circumspect behavior that Jacob was nervous about something, but he didn't press him to find out what it was.

The *bar-mitzvah* itself went smoothly. Very little was expected of Jacob, and that suited him just fine. Because Skalat traditionally honored the father on the day of his son's *bar-mitzvah* more than the son, Zvi Hersh read the *Haftorah* in the morning, while Jacob received his first *aliyah* to the Torah at *Minchah*. Zvi Hersh also prepared a large reception in the *shul* after *Shacharis*.

The next Monday, Zvi Hersh called Jacob to his side. "Now that you are *bar-mitzvah*, I am going to entrust you with more important duties than before."

"I will do whatever Tatte asks of me," Jacob dutifully answered.

"I want you to take this two hundred dollars in American money to Tarnapol. You are to go to the stamp office there and tell the clerk I sent you. They will know what to give you in return for the money. You are then to return to me, and I will pay you for the day's work."

Father and son would both later claim that they looked at each other a little more closely than usual. It was a scrutiny well-warranted, because they were never to see each other again.

The next day, Sarah Elfenbein delivered a letter to Shimon and Faige that Jacob had left with her.

Dear Shimon and Faige,

I have rehearsed this routine so often, and now I am actually carrying it out. By the time Faige's sister delivers this letter to you, I should be on my way to Berlin. From there, I plan to take a train to Belgium, and then I will go to the sea coast. I hope that I will not have to wait too long for a ship to America, but I'll wait as long as I have to.

I'm not sure how long my money will last. If necessary, I'll work until I have the money that I need to get to Tante Frieda. I planned to leave for America on the same day that Tatte gave me the money for the stamps. Of course, I never expected him to send me on an errand with money in my hand. The money seemed like it was sent by Heaven. Imagine being given two hundred dollars in American money on the very day that I had planned to leave! I had enough saved for the train trip to Berlin, but I didn't know what I would do when I got there. Of course, I plan one day to return the money to him.

Heaven bless you both. Shimon, I'll always love you as my big brother. Regards to my father and sisters. The next letter will be from America.

Much love,
Jacob

P.S. Shimon, you don't have to worry about my throwing my *tefillin* overboard when I set out to sea—I never took them with me.

Shimon read the letter out loud to Faige. Then he folded it carefully. "I guess I ought to show it to Tatte."

Zvi Hersh was quiet as Shimon read the letter to him. He winced at the mention of the *tefillin* left behind, but he made no comment. After what seemed like a long silence, he turned to Shimon. "It would seem that I finally did something good for Jacob."

Shimon was astonished. Did his father send Jacob for the stamps because he knew that he was going to leave home for America with very little money? Shimon had to ask.

"You will never really know," his father answered. "You will never really know."

# CHAPTER 8

★

Shimon and Faige received their next letter from Jacob in the fall of 1910, almost a year after he had left. Shimon ripped open the envelope and read the letter out loud.

Dear Faige and Shimon,

I can't believe that it has been a year since I wrote you my good-bye letter when I left Skalat. So much has happened since then. But first things first. I have sent you a bank money order for two hundred dollars for Tatte's money that I borrowed from him. You can take it to the American consulate in Tarnapol and get money for it. That is the way they do things in America. Please give the money to Tatte and explain to him that I did not steal it, I only borrowed it.

I had trouble writing you this letter. Of course, it had to be in Yiddish, though, as you know, my Yiddish was never that good. I'm learning English now four nights a week. I finally found a rabbi who was able to write this letter from my dictation.

The trip to Belgium was exciting. When I got there, I felt that if I turned around and returned immediately I would have already seen more than I would have had I stayed in Skalat. On my way to Belgium, I spent a day in Berlin. I couldn't believe the tall buildings and the wide streets. Luckily, I had some extra money. They don't treat strangers there the way we do in Skalat. I could have stayed there a month and nobody would have known I was there.

I got to Belgium in early October and bought a shipscard to leave for America on October 15. I was lucky; that was almost the last scheduled ship for the winter. I loved the trip to America, but many people found it hard. The ship was crowded, and I went the cheapest way, which they call steerage. It entitles you to nothing but a boarding pass. I had to provide my own meals and find my own place to sleep. It was no problem. I followed your example and brought a big salami, some other foods and lots of bread.

The people on the boat were very nice, and everyone was happy to be going to America. There were many Jewish people on the ship from all parts of Europe, but mostly from Russia. There was a lot of singing and dancing, but many people got sick. They call it seasickness. Families even cooked meals on the decks of the ship. I was afraid they would burn up the boat, but nothing bad happened.

The trip took almost six weeks. We pulled into New York harbor around the first of December. They have a statue in the harbor that they call the Statue of Liberty. When we saw it, people began to shout, sing and cry. Strangers rejoiced together, sharing their excitement. After that, we were told that we could leave the boat at Ellis Island. There they went over our papers, and we were given physical examinations. Some people were selected to be examined more closely. It was very confusing. Every language you can think of was spoken in the hall.

While I was sitting on a bench in the entrance room, Shmuel Gross came up to me. I couldn't believe it. After all this time, there he was, as he said he would be, ready to help me get settled in America. He's been in America less than a year, and he speaks English already. He cut off his beard and was wearing a suit with a short jacket. I don't know how I could have done without him. We left for Tante Frieda's house in Jersey City that same day. I was amazed at everything. Shmuel kept laughing and saying that I was acting like a "greenhorn." I didn't know then what a "greenhorn" was, but they use the word a lot around here. It means the latest person to come to America. We had to go through New York to get to Jersey City. They have trains that run under the ground. They call them subways.

Tante Frieda and the entire Gross family were very nice to me. I feel that I will owe them a part of me forever. They made a party for me. Tante has six of her sons, all of them married, living near her. She lives with her daughter, son-in-law and their children in an apartment over the store. Tante explained to me that there were already too many people making a living out of the store. I was to stay there for a while until I got some of the "green" out of me.

After I was there a month or so, the Grosses began to talk to a salesman about a job for me. He sells them dairy goods. They asked him to give me a job. He goes around to different stores and sells butter, eggs, cheeses and all sorts of dairy items. The man's name is Mr. Fischer. He has a big business in Newark that he had just started, and he needed salesmen. Mr. Fischer hired me. He pays me $5 a week plus 5% commission of my sales over $50. I have been in this country less than a year, and I'm already making more money than a lot of people that I know. I run around all day long to every grocery I can think of, even to some stores far from the warehouse.

I work long hours, but I love it. I'm always working by seven in the morning and never finish before seven at night. Then Monday, Tuesday, Wednesday and Thursday I go to school. You'll be happy to know that I don't work on Saturday, not because I don't want to, but because that is the stores' biggest selling day. They don't want to see a salesman on Saturday. But I normally go to the warehouse and look over all the things they want to sell. We also have our sales meeting on that day.

I live in a boarding house on Prince Street, one of the important streets where all newcomers to America live. I love America, I love my work, and I'm doing very well. They say I'm a natural-born salesman. All I know is that I like people, and I try to figure out how they can make money if they buy their butter and eggs from me. I even learned how to arrange displays for them so that they will sell more.

This is the longest letter I have ever written, but I wanted to tell you just how wonderful everything is. When the day comes for you both to come to America, you have nothing to worry about. I will do everything for you that Tante and her family did for me, and more. You will not have to borrow $200.

Lots of love to the whole family. Please tell them how well I am doing and that I love them very much. Would you believe that here I am, only fourteen years old, and people are trying to get me married? I look older than my age; I'm already five foot ten inches and growing. You better watch out, Shimon—maybe I'll be taller than you some day.

All my love,
Jacob

Shimon folded the letter and looked at Faige. "Did you hear that, Faige? The boy is fourteen years old, he's been in America less than a year, and already he's a successful businessman."

"But look what happened to him. He doesn't even keep *Shabbos* any more."

Shimon was silent for a few long moments.

"I'm not really surprised," he finally said. "But what could you expect? Look at how he behaved in Skalat. He never went to *cheder*. He didn't even take his *tefillin* with him."

"I still think it's terrible. What's the use of making money in America, if you give up everything that's important? But you're right. Jacob was headed that way even here in Poland." She shrugged. "Well, at the rate he's going he'll probably end up getting married soon."

In September, 1912, three years after she and Shimon had been married, Faige gave birth to a baby boy.

The family was elated. Faige and Shimon named their son Kalman Yosef, after the baby's maternal grandfather, Rabbi Kalman Yosef Shapiro.

The world was in a turmoil when little Kalman was born. The Balkan Wars of 1912-1913 had pushed the world closer to the precipice of 1914, the beginning of World War I. The Turks attempted to hold together what was left of the Ottoman Empire, while the Balkan League was formed to resist them. On October 8, 1912, Montenegro declared war on Turkey. Bulgaria, Greece and Serbia followed suit immediately. The remnant of Turkey was completely vanquished.

Rumors teemed throughout Skalat. The Poles, it was said, would certainly make a determined drive for their own statehood. Captain Rosenkranz was dispatched to the easternmost front and ordered to stop any invasion from that boundary. Rosenkranz's successor was ordered to beef up the Austrian military in Skalat.

In his capacity as a member of the city council, Zvi Hersh saw the list of inductees to the Austrian army first. His heart sank when he saw that it carried Shimon's name. He was to be inducted again into the cavalry with his old rank and duties.

An alarmed Zvi Hersh decided he had to talk to Rosenkranz about Shimon. His message was clearly too sensitive to entrust to anyone else, and he resolved to ride to the front at night, alone. It was a short but dangerous trip.

When Zvi Hersh entered the camp, he asked to see Captain Rosenkranz and was escorted to him. Rosenkranz was amazed to see him.

"I don't believe that you came here like this. It shows the laxity of my men that you weren't killed. What could possibly be that urgent?"

After Zvi Hersh told him about his son's imminent induction, Captain Rosenkranz laughed heartily.

"There is nothing I can do about this one, Herr Halevy. Shimon will most certainly be taken. Vienna is in a severe crisis, and they are very serious about strengthening the army. You can't buy a substitute either. The records show that he has already had army training, and he is exactly the type of man they want."

Zvi Hersh interrupted with a desperate reminder. "He'll be killed, you know."

"Of course," confirmed Rosenkranz, "and he'll never know if the bullet came from in front or in back of him. There are still people who want to see him killed. There is nothing I can do. You had better leave, Herr Halevy; just standing here talking to you puts me in a bad light. I'll have some of my men escort you back to Skalat."

Zvi Hersh rode home in the company of two soldiers. During the silent journey, Zvi Hersh considered the options Shimon had. He made up his mind that Shimon would have to leave for America. There was no other way to avoid conscription and almost certain death.

He confronted Shimon with his idea the next day. Shimon told his father he would have to discuss it with Faige. When Faige heard about the plan, she was indignant.

"Why should I go to America?" she implored. "We have a son less than a year old. The business is doing well. It doesn't make any sense. I know things seem bad right now, but I'm sure they will change. We're just beginning to settle down. I couldn't just pick up and leave."

"I assure you, Faige, this is not my idea. I don't know what we should do. I'm only trying to talk it over with you. Tatte saw my name on the induction list. He spoke to Rosenkranz about it, and Rosenkranz can't help us. I don't care very much about myself. Others have gone to war. Some die, and some survive. That's in Heaven's hands. I'm trying to think of you and our son and do what is best for us. Tatte and Rosenkranz feel that I have too many enemies to survive the scenario."

"So look at the choice I have—a dead husband or a husband on the other side of the world!"

Shimon looked startled. "What do you mean by that? I'm not going to go by myself. You'll come with me."

Faige shook her head. "I can't. I just know that I couldn't survive the trip with Kalman. I can't take that chance."

"So what do we do?" Shimon asked.

"Why don't we wait to see what happens instead of having you leave to America immediately? In the meantime, you should write to Jacob and let him know your situation. I'm sure he'll send you a shipscard. That will take months, but so will your induction. The army always gives you time to set your affairs in order after they call you. That way we won't have to rush into anything."

Shimon decided to adopt Faige's plan; after all, it bought time, and he could see what would develop in the next few months. They carefully drafted a letter to Jacob that evening and mailed it the following day.

A peace treaty was signed in London between Turkey and the Balkan states in May of 1913, but instead of defusing the many disputes in the area, the truce seemed to incite further fighting. It was clear that the Austro-Hungarian Empire, because of its vast interests in the area, would be impressed into conflict over the territory. Germany's unconditional support of Austria would spread the war to all of Europe.

The recruitment list Zvi Hersh had seen was tabled by the treaty. Shimon began to entertain advice to leave immediately, before the list was published anew. If he waited and left after he would received his orders, he was told, he could be accused of deserting the Austrian army. But Shimon still didn't leave.

Towards the end of the summer, Shimon and Faige finally received the long-awaited reply from Jacob. "Yes, come immediately. Everybody in America believes that there will be a war in Europe."

The letter contained a shipscard and a bank money order for two hundred dollars. "You should not have to wait for Tatte to send you for stamps," Jacob wrote.

Shimon immediately notified his father of Jacob's letter. Zvi Hersh handed him an envelope. "Here is two hundred dollars for your trip. I seem to do this for my sons as they leave Skalat. I don't expect to see Jacob again, but your case is different. You will be leaving a wife and son here, so if I live, we'll see each other again. I think you ought to go immediately after *Rosh Hashanah* and not wait for *Yom Kippur*. The induction list is due to be published any day."

Zvi Hersh embraced his son. "May the Almighty be with you."

Shimon left Skalat two days after *Rosh Hashanah*. He took his cherished *tallis* and *tefillin*, very little clothing, a shipscard and fifty dollars in American money. A still-weeping Faige discovered three hundred and fifty dollars in the cash box after he left. Her sister Sarah Elfenbein was with her.

"Tell me, Faige, why didn't you go with him?"

"I'm pregnant with our second child," Faige disclosed. "I didn't tell Shimon. He never would have gone if he had known."

# CHAPTER 9

★

*S*himon stood apprehensively in the Tarnapol station and waited for the train that would take him to Berlin. Between glances at the clock, he noticed two men he recognized from Skalat. Mordechai Ehrens was a *shochet*, and Yosef Kagan *davened* in the same *shul* as Shimon. Each looked at the bundles the other was carrying and began to laugh.

"It looks like we're all going on a long trip," Shimon remarked.

"I'm going to America," Mordechai volunteered. He explained that he was marked for induction into the Austrian army. He was married with a three-year-old son, and his wife insisted that he try to save himself.

Yosef hadn't been conscripted but had been unable to earn a living in Skalat. He and his wife of two years were childless and decided that Yosef should try his luck elsewhere. Yosef promised to return to Skalat within two years, rich or poor.

Shimon was glad to have the company of fellow townsmen,

and the three decided to arrange their travel plans together. On their way to Berlin, they agreed to continue on from there to Frankfurt-am-Main, where they would spend the remaining six days until *Yom Kippur*. It was a city renowned for helping Jewish travelers, and the hospitality of the people belonging to the *shul* of Rabbi Samson Raphael Hirsch was legendary.

When they reached Berlin, the three men were overwhelmed by what they saw. The city, with its tall buildings and wide boulevards, was by far the largest they had ever seen. The people seemed endlessly en route to unknown destinations. And much to their surprise, it was difficult to distinguish Jew from gentile.

"I wouldn't even know how to go about finding the Jewish community in Berlin," Mordechai commented. "All the people dress alike, and the *shul*s and churches look the same."

Shimon agreed. For the first time, he felt that his long coat placed him in a quaint minority. Confused and uneasy, the three chose to leave Berlin the day they arrived.

When they reached the Frankfurt station by train, the men were uncertain as to how to proceed. Since Mordechai spoke German the best, he approached the first policeman he saw in the station.

"I beg your pardon, Mein Herr," he began timidly. "Could you be kind enough to direct us to the synagogue of Rabbi Samson Raphael Hirsch?"

"I don't know where synagogues are," the policeman answered curtly. "There are usually Jews who hang around outside the station to take care of people like you. Go look for them."

Shimon quickly led the way towards the exit. As they stepped into the street, they noticed a crowd of a dozen Germans circling a Jew wearing a long black coat, black beard and earlocks.

"Our Jews in Frankfurt don't dress like this any more," a tall, heavy-set man with red hair taunted the Jew. "If you want to stay here, we'll have to teach you how to dress."

Shimon edged nervously towards the crowd. He noticed two bearded men in short, black jackets trying to reason with the redhead.

"He just arrived," they pleaded. "Please let him go. He's coming with us."

"Why do they always come here?" complained the redhead, who apparently was the ringleader. "I'm sick of seeing these Jews coming to our town. We've had enough of them."

By now, Shimon and his friends had reached the group. Shimon waited until one of the ruffians struck the Jew before he acted. He pushed his way into the crowd and stepped into the center.

"I also dress the same way," he said, looking around at the hostile faces. "Why don't one of you pick a fight with me instead?"

The ringleader roared with laughter. "Do you hear that, fellows? The Jew is challenging us. Now this is getting interesting. I accept, unless someone else feels strongly about it."

He turned to Shimon and abruptly tried to trip him. But Shimon was too fast. He jumped to avoid his opponent and took advantage of the man's unsteadiness, hitting him with all his strength in the face. The fight was over. The man was left on the sidewalk, hurt and humiliated.

To Shimon's amazement, everyone, including the attacker's friends, applauded him. Startled, Shimon bent down to lift up the injured man.

"You don't have to do that, Jew," the redhead said, pushing Shimon away. "I can accept defeat, but I'd love to know where you learned how to fight."

Before Shimon could respond, one of the bearded men approached him.

"We better go before this gets out of hand," he said in a

hurry. "I assume you're looking for the Hirsch *shul*."

Shimon and his friends followed the German Jews to the Jewish quarter, accompanied by the man Shimon had just saved. His name was Velvel Mandel, a Russian who was also en route to America.

The four were placed with four different host families. They were provided with food and sleeping arrangements until they could resume their travels.

The day after *Yom Kippur*, the group set out for Belgium. The *shul* paid for Velvel's ticket and offered Shimon money as well. Shimon refused. He felt he could not accept community funds unless he was absolutely destitute, and he could still afford his fare.

Before boarding the train, they were given the name of a man in Belgium to contact should they need help. When they reached Belgium, they learned they had just missed a boat to America by two days. The next ship was not to set sail for another month. This left Shimon in a strange city without any money, having spent it all on train fares.

All the same, Shimon was not worse off than his companions. He at least had his shipscard, so he did not have to worry about paying for a ticket. Mordechai and Yosef had money but no idea how much they would have to pay for their passage. Velvel had neither money nor a shipscard.

The small group contacted the man whose name they had been given in Frankfurt. He was a pleasant elderly Jew, who helped get the four settled. Each man was given lodging in a boarding house but told that, since community funds were short, he would have to work while he stayed in Belgium. This actually pleased all four. They did not want to extend the community any more than necessary, and the work would also help pass the time.

When the date of their departure finally arrived, Shimon

and his friends eagerly lined up on the ship's docks along with other passengers travelling in steerage, which was the cheapest travelling section. Most of the passengers carried their belongings in bags or boxes; few had valises. Shimon saw entire families huddled together. Children were crying, and parents tried in vain to restore their spirits.

"It doesn't look like it's going to be an easy trip," Shimon said to Mordechai as he set down his bag for the wait. His bag was weighed down by the food he had brought along. Most of the Jewish emigrants shunned the *treif* food the ship stocked and resorted to the breads and meats they brought on board. Shimon had taken six breads, two huge salamis and a bottle of *schnapps* for his voyage.

"I don't care how difficult this trip will be," Mordechai responded. "We're going to America!"

The trip did turn out to be difficult. During the voyage, many people were seasick, and the smell of vomit pervaded the rooms. Most of the young men avoided the rooms and stayed on deck almost all of the time, including sleeping hours. Shimon and his new friends spent their time on the deck in endless talk and speculation about the new world they were approaching.

The anxiety Shimon had felt earlier at having left Faige and Kalman alone seemed to dissipate into the very winds that carried the ship. He was imbued with the excitement and enthusiasm that permeated the air aboard the boat and which transformed the ordinary traveller into an adventurer.

One morning, towards the end of the six-week journey, Shimon caught sight of the Statue of Liberty in the distance. Still wearing his *tallis* and *tefillin*, he quickly finished *davening* and rushed to his companions.

"Did you see the Statue of Liberty?" he shouted. "Did you see it? It's enormous! It fills up a whole island!"

As they stood and watched, the legendary statue grew larger and larger in the morning mist. She seemed to reach out to each and every one of them, beckoning them to share in the boundless opportunities of the New World and gently coaxing them to leave the weary baggage of their former lives behind.

They soon learned that they were finally in New York harbor and would disembark at Ellis Island that day. Few, including Shimon, had dry eyes.

Amidst all the excitement and ebullience, Shimon resolved silently that, no matter what the future held in store, he would remain loyal to the religion and traditions of his ancestors. He would not work on *Shabbos*, he would pray every day, and he would only eat kosher food. The thought of how he might someday bring up his children in such an environment did not cross his mind at the time.

# CHAPTER 10

★

*S*himon and his friends silently came off the barges at Ellis Island and walked up the quay into the main building. While watching the mob depart from the ship, the finality of his arrival overwhelmed Shimon. Over and over he asked himself what he was doing here. How had he allowed himself to leave Faige and Kalman in Skalat while he turned into a wanderer? What price would this throbbing new land exact from him? He was not the unencumbered thirteen-year-old Jacob had been when he had made the same crossing four years ago. He was twenty-seven years old, with a wife and a child and an ancient way of life that he cherished.

Shimon got so caught up in his thoughts that Mordechai had to shout to direct him to the Great Hall at the top of the stairs. When he reached it, Shimon thought to himself that the room was aptly named. It was an enormous chamber with wooden benches arranged in rows across the room. An official at the head of the stairs motioned the arrivals to follow the stream of traffic toward the examining rooms. None of the three was detained for a special examination.

Next, Shimon was assigned to a wooden bench to wait for the legal inspection, which consisted of the same questions asked when the shipscard was purchased.

Shimon sat on the bench, stunned by the speed with which he was being handled and worried about the impending inspection. Since Jacob had bought the shipscard for him in New York, Jacob had answered the questions for him. Shimon had no idea how he would answer them.

He moved forward on the bench and strained to hear what the inspector was asking the other immigrants. As he did so, he saw a handsome, well-dressed man walking towards him. Shimon almost jumped from his seat. He couldn't believe his eyes. It was Jacob!

Seventeen-year-old Jacob strode forward to meet Shimon with the confidence and appearance of a much older man. He wore a gray, pinstriped suit, a maroon tie, dark socks that spired almost up to his knees and expensive-looking shoes. When the two brothers embraced, Shimon hugged a boy he hardly knew.

"Jacob, I barely recognized you," Shimon finally managed to say.

"I'm certainly not the same person you remember," Jacob agreed. He turned to the legal inspector. "I'll answer any questions for him. This is my brother."

As the two shook hands, Shimon thought he saw dollar bills pass from Jacob's hand to the inspector's. The inspection didn't take long after that. The inspector went through the questions in two minutes, addressing only Jacob, who acknowledged his replies by nodding his head.

"You're free to go now," the inspector concluded.

"Come," Jacob directed Shimon. "Let's get your things, and I'll take you to the Gross house. They're expecting you."

Shimon looked around anxiously. He didn't want to leave without saying good-bye to Mordechai and Yosef. Fortunately, Shimon noticed Mordechai's large figure three rows to his left, and ran to his side.

"I found my brother, and we're leaving now," he told Mordechai. "Where do you plan to go?"

"You said your brother lives in Newark," Mordechai said, clutching his belongings in his hands. "It makes little difference to me. I'll go to Newark, too. Yosef will probably come with me. Where should we meet there?"

"I've heard of the Russian Shul in Newark," Shimon answered, relieved that he would have his friends nearby. "Leave your name there, and I'll find you."

Shimon ran back to Jacob and followed him to the ferry that would take them from Ellis Island to Manhattan. From there, they took the Hudson Tubes to Jersey City. Shimon's first ride on an underground train astonished him, as did the haste and orderliness of the passengers. Everyone seemed in a hurry, yet accustomed to the delays and bustle of public transportation.

Shimon was grateful to have Jacob with him. At the same time, he was beginning to realize that his relationship with his brother would never be the same as it had been in Skalat. Shimon noticed how Jacob had looked at his beard and long coat in a condescending manner. Jacob was no longer the admiring, younger brother, and Shimon sensed that Jacob discerned the difference, too.

When the brothers arrived at Tante Frieda's house, Shimon was completely overcome by the Gross's hospitality. It was *Chanukah*, and the entire family was gathered together. They all tried their best to make Shimon feel comfortable.

Shimon was appreciative but also uneasy. Tante Frieda's appearance was unnerving. She looked so much like his deceased mother that the resemblance was very painful, and the family merriment and glowing candles only intensified his loneliness. Shimon was in America less than a day, and he was already homesick.

When Jacob and Shimon finally left the Gross house, it was almost midnight. They took the Hudson Tubes to Newark, and Shimon marvelled at how many people were still travelling so late at night.

"Do the trains always run this late?" Shimon asked.

"In America, the trains run all night," Jacob answered.

After a ten-minute ride, Jacob led Shimon across a wide street where they waited for the first of two trolley rides. After slightly more than a half hour, the two stood in front of Jacob's boarding house.

"You're welcome to stay here as long as you want," Jacob said, unlocking the door and leading Shimon into his room. "This is one of the more established boarding houses in the area. They charge me four dollars a week, and they have their own bathrooms. There is one on this floor down the hall, but it gets very busy in the morning."

Shimon looked around Jacob's room. A cot had been placed beside the three-quarter bed for Shimon's use. There was an ice box, a table and two wooden chairs in one corner. In the other was a table, chair and lamp. The room was neat and looked like it received regular cleaning services.

Shimon thanked his brother and set down the meager bundle he had brought with him from Skalat. How odd it looked in this strange new setting, Shimon thought.

Jacob continued talking to Shimon as the two got ready for bed. "I usually get up around six o'clock in the morning, and I'm out of the house by seven. I like to start my day early, because that's the best time to see my customers. They get busy later in the day and don't want to talk. If you want anything, you have to go to Prince Street. You'll find everything there."

Before turning off the light, Jacob took out some money and left it on the table. "Here is ten dollars. That's what the average worker makes in a week, so it should last you for a while. If you need more money, I'll give it to you."

Shimon thanked Jacob and lay down on his cot, trying to absorb all the information he just received. His mind wandered back to Skalat. He thought about Faige and Kalman and wondered what they were doing now. The realization that he was finally in America made him miss his family all the more. He continued thinking of them until weariness finally overtook him, and he fell asleep.

# CHAPTER 11

★

*S*himon woke up the next morning and stared at the rose pattern in the aging wallpaper of the small room. Jacob had already left, and Shimon felt uneasy in his new surroundings. He lay on the cot for a few minutes, vaguely contemplating the wallpaper and wondering what the day had in store for him. Then he got up.

By seven o'clock, Shimon had stationed himself on the corner of Prince and Mercer Streets with his *tallis* and *tefillin* bag in hand. Even among the scurrying masses of people dressed in typical American fashion, Prince Street was still home to men like Shimon, in long coat and full beard. He touched one such person on the arm and asked him where he could find a *shul*.

"Oh, there are many *shuls* in this area," the man replied, surveying Shimon's appearance. "Tell me, what part of Europe do you come from?"

"I come from Skalat, in Galicia. It's now part of the Austro-Hungarian Empire."

"Ahh," the man said smilingly. "You want the Morton Street Shul. Go two blocks straight to Barclay Street, then turn left for two blocks. On the corner of Barclay and Morton Streets you will see a *shul*. Just follow the street signs."

"Street signs?" Shimon asked sheepishly.

The man laughed. "This must be your first day in America. Street signs are the circular steel rods on every corner. They have signs on top that tell you the name of the street. You see this one here? It says 'Prince Street' in one direction and 'Mercer Street' in another."

Shimon stared up in wonder. He had been so taken by the paved streets and sidewalks that he hadn't even noticed the poles. He thanked the man and headed down Prince Street, glancing in awe in every direction.

Even the most energetic market day in Skalat had never churned with such dynamism. The noise of the people and traffic sounded like a continuous clamor. Pedestrians, bicyclists, horse-drawn wagons and cars jammed the streets. Shops were opening, their owners festooning their windows with wares and installing signs in English and Yiddish. The shopgirls bustled about in colorful print dresses, so vibrant compared to the subdued colors worn by their contemporaries in Europe.

By the time Shimon reached the *shul,* a big, domed brick building, he was a few minutes late for *Shacharis.* He walked in through the side door, trying to make as little disturbance as possible.

Shimon looked around while he *davened,* struck by the size and grandeur of the *shul.* The *davening,* however, was comforting in its familiarity, an authentic, if transient, suggestion of home. After *davening,* the *shammash* welcomed Shimon and assured him he could leave his *tallis* bag for the following day.

It was just before eight when Shimon left the *shul* and walked onto Prince Street. A vegetable merchant was opening his store, positioning piles of beans, squash and oranges while juggling a container of coffee and a buttered roll. Next door, a man carried plates, pots and jars outside his store to the sidewalk stands.

At a haberdashery, Shimon heard a man yelling at his employee.

"No, no!" he shouted. "Don't put the sweaters over there. We had them there yesterday, and we didn't sell any. Keep the sweaters inside today. Let's try jackets here. Bring me three or four jackets from inside."

Shimon paused in front of the store. He stood for a few minutes, blocking part of the sidewalk.

"Can I do anything for you?" asked the haberdasher in Yiddish.

Shimon thought for a long moment before speaking. "Do you have a short jacket in my size?"

"Of course we do," the man answered. "I would say you wear about a size 42 long. Try this on, and we'll take it from there."

Within seconds of his request, Shimon was centered in front of a tall mirror, studying himself in the strange garment. He liked the updated image that reflected back at him and remembered the disdainful look Jacob had given his appearance at Ellis Island. But he couldn't help thinking of the number of times he had ridiculed such clothes.

"How much does it cost?" Shimon asked, half-hoping to hear an exorbitant price.

"I should get five dollars for it," the man answered. "But I can tell that you're new in this country. Fewer and fewer people are wearing these long coats you have. They just feel out of place here, so I'll give you the coat for four dollars."

"I have a problem, though," Shimon said hesitatingly. "Even my long coat is too cold for your American weather. How am I going to manage with a short jacket?"

The man had heard it all before.

"That's no problem," he assured his customer. "You'll buy an overcoat from me for another four dollars. For a total of eight dollars you look good, you're warm, and you're on your way to becoming a real American."

"I can't afford eight dollars," Shimon said, taking off the coat.

"Tell me, how much are you able to afford?" the owner persisted.

"I can give you five for both the jacket and the coat."

"Done," the man replied. "And just to complete the good deed I'm doing for you, I'll give you a decent hat for nothing. You can't wear that old hat with your new clothes."

Had Jacob done the bargaining, Shimon would have had the outfit for three-fifty, but Shimon thought he had gotten a bargain. A bit bewildered, he walked out of the store in his new jacket, coat, hat and self. A bag stored the wardrobe he had just replaced, but the doubts were not as easily discarded. I'll still wear my long coat on *Shabbos*, he rationalized.

As Shimon headed back onto the main street, he heard someone coming up behind him.

"Hey, Shimon, is that you?" exclaimed the man. It was Mordechai. "I can't believe it, you of all people in a short jacket? I didn't even recognize you! Next thing you know you'll cut off your beard."

Shimon explained his uneasiness around Jacob in his European dress, justifying his new image as much to himself as to Mordechai.

"Well, while you've been busy buying clothes, I've been inquiring about work. From what I hear, America has the same need for a good *shochet* that Belgium had. I don't think I'll have any trouble finding a job."

Mordechai shifted his huge frame and stroked his beard.

"You know Shimon, I think we made a big mistake by not bringing our families with us."

Shimon didn't answer. From the little he had seen on Prince Street that morning, he had already sensed the magnitude of opportunities available in this new world. But he knew he was not here to stay and didn't want to get caught up in enthusiasm for his temporary home.

Before parting, he made plans with Mordechai to spend their first *Shabbos* together at Lustbader's, the kosher boarding house where Mordechai and Yosef were staying. The rest of the day Shimon spent walking on Prince Street, marvelling at the sights and familiarizing himself with the area.

That evening, Shimon was met by another startled reaction from Jacob.

"Where did you get that outfit?" Jacob asked in astonishment, as he eyed his brother's clothing.

"Do you like it?"

"It's certainly an improvement," Jacob said.

The next morning, the members of the Morton Street Shul were taken aback, too.

"Lucky we had a chance to see you yesterday," one man said. "Otherwise, we wouldn't know who you really are."

"I haven't changed anything except my appearance," Shimon insisted. "I still intend to pray three times a day."

Shimon was true to his pledge. He didn't miss *davening* and showed up in *shul* that *Erev Shabbos* in his long coat. After *davening*, he joined Mordechai and Yosef at Lustbader's.

Shimon had been anxious the past two days to tell Jacob of his plans to stay at Lustbader's for *Shabbos*. He didn't want to insult Jacob by not staying with him. But Jacob appeared relieved when Shimon told him.

"I don't observe *Shabbos* by your standards, Shimon," Jacob told him. "We have a sales meeting Saturday morning, and then

I have conferences. Sometimes the boss invites me to lunch at his house, but it's not what you would call a *Shabbos* meal. You're probably better off with your friends."

Jacob was right. Shimon's first *Shabbos* in Newark was remarkable and enjoyable. Remarkable, because in form and content it was no different than any *Shabbos* he had experienced in Skalat. The *davening* at *shul* was the same, and even some of the congregants looked like they could have been from Skalat.

Lustbader's was a pleasant place to spend *Shabbos*. The food was simple but ample. Tables had been set aside on the second floor for those residents of the boarding house who wanted to eat *Shabbos* meals. It amused Shimon that they were enjoying a *Shabbos* meal above a tavern that was open for business at the same time.

The three friends marvelled at how much had happened in the four days since they had arrived. Mordechai had found a job as a *shochet*, and Yosef was selling tuna fish for a local merchant.

"Are you working yet?" Yosef asked Shimon.

"No, I guess that I'm not as successful as you and Mordechai," Shimon replied without rancor.

"Well, Shimon," Mordechai commented, "you have been busy buying clothes."

# CHAPTER 12

★

*B*y August of 1914, the nations of Europe found themselves immersed in war. For Shimon, his safe distance from the fighting did not spare him the suffering. The thought of Faige and Kalman alone in wartime Skalat was almost unbearable, and the notion that he had deserted his wife and child in such conditions plagued his conscience unremittingly.

Shimon was fighting another battle as well. In quick succession, Shimon found work in three different grocery stores and failed at each.

He began to work for his cousin Martin Gross and his wife Lena in their grocery store in Jersey City. Shimon enjoyed the work, and the familial ambience of a husband-and-wife tandem seemed natural to him. The working day lasted until seven at night, but he did not object to the twelve-hour day.

The problem began on Friday afternoon. Seeing that no one had talked to him about the approaching *Shabbos*, Shimon began to undo his apron.

"Where do you think you're going?" Martin asked.

"Home," Shimon replied. "If I don't leave now, I'll never make it in time for *Shabbos.*"

"You're kidding," Martin said. "You don't really think that you can observe *Shabbos* in America, do you?"

"Martin, when I came to work here, you didn't mention that I would be expected to work on *Shabbos.*"

"I wouldn't have imagined that you would expect not to work on *Shabbos,*" Martin said in an exasperated tone. "Look, Shimon, I do about thirty percent of my entire week's business on Saturday. Some stores have a decent Sunday business, but we don't. The Poles who live around here don't shop on Sunday because they go to church. I couldn't close on Saturday even if I wanted to."

Shimon looked at the floor, not knowing what to say. He didn't see why he should sacrifice his Saturday so that the Poles could observe their Sunday, but didn't think Martin would be interested in his argument.

"I guess you ought to go home now," Martin said, rather apologetically. "I don't want you to do anything that you couldn't live with. You're a good worker and I like you, but you can't stay here without working on Saturday."

"I didn't expect it to end like this," Shimon said.

"I didn't either, Shimon," Martin admitted. "I suggest you try one of my brothers Louis in New Brunswick or Norman in Elizabeth. Their stores aren't as large as mine. Perhaps you can work something out with them."

Shimon said good-bye to Lena and headed straight home. He arrived at Lustbader's at the last possible moment before *Shabbos.*

Lustbader's had recently become Shimon's home. The week before, Shimon had left Jacob's boarding house to live there with Mordechai and Yosef. Shimon had felt uncomfortable living off Jacob for free and was more at ease living with his friends. A permanent bed was added to Mordechai's and Yosef's room, and Shimon paid the same dollar-fifty per week they paid.

The Monday after his failed job with Martin, Shimon took the train to New Brunswick to Louis Gross's grocery. Here, *Shabbos* posed no problem, but his accommodations did. Louis had just married and his young wife Sarah worked with him. Because of the long distance separating Newark and New Brunswick, Shimon was given a room in their apartment during the week. But he found it impossible to live there, continually feeling like an intruder. The parting was completely amiable, and Louis and Sarah remained good friends with their ex-employee.

At Norman's store in Elizabeth, Shimon again had no problem leaving early on Fridays. The hours, however, were long, and no direct bus or train connected Elizabeth and Newark. As a rule, he would not return from work until eleven at night. Shimon quit as politely as he could.

After failing with the Gross family, Shimon tried work with a cousin from his father's side of the family. Some of his father's relatives had moved to America years before and had just recently formed a commercial window-cleaning business. One of his cousins, Isadore Feresh, urged Shimon to work with him.

The two men set out with pails of water, a sack of rags and long poles that held sponges and wipers. It was still dark at five in the morning when they began their walk toward their early jobs in downtown Newark. Many customers specified that the windows be cleaned before working hours so that it not interfere with their business.

The window-cleaning business worked out well. For three days, it looked as if Shimon had finally found himself. He enjoyed the work on deserted main streets, and he liked working outdoors, feeling invigorated by the cold, fresh air. As a bonus, he enjoyed Isadore's company.

The problem occurred on Wednesday, when they scheduled their work for the remainder of the week. Shimon stood stunned into silence as Isadore showed him their *Shabbos* regimen. He couldn't believe the problem had recurred.

"I thought you knew, Isadore," Shimon said. "I can't work on *Shabbos*."

"I don't believe it!" Isadore exclaimed. "You're going to try to live that way in America? No one does."

Shimon didn't want to argue. He mumbled a few words of gratitude to his cousin for giving him a chance and told him he would have to look for something else.

That evening, Shimon recounted his experience to Yosef and Mordechai.

"I don't understand it," he said. "Does everybody work on *Shabbos* in America?"

"I don't," Mordechai said.

"Neither do I," Yosef contended. "I think that the problems you've been going through are ridiculous. All the jobs you had were no good in the first place. You never made more than seven-fifty per week, and that was for long hours. I am making more than that now, plus I'm building my own business at the same time. And I make my own hours."

Yosef paused for a moment and looked at Shimon.

"Selling isn't for everyone," he admitted. "But I'm willing to let you try working with me if that would help you."

Shimon was overwhelmed with gratitude. He began working with Yosef the following day and tried to follow Yosef's mode of selling. Like Jacob, Yosef was a born salesman. He staked his faith in his product and had no problem soliciting customers for it.

Shimon was very different. He became flustered when he

entered a stranger's establishment and felt awkward with the staff, which quickly perceived his discomfort. In addition, he became increasingly dispirited by his dearth of sales and commissions.

"I don't understand," Yosef said. "Didn't you and Faige run a store in Skalat?"

"That was different. Our customers there were friends and neighbors. I had no problems selling to them. Here, you have to do business with people you don't know."

Shimon told Yosef he would look around for something else and finally found a position that he was to keep until he returned to Skalat.

Friends at Lustbader's had told Shimon of a new ketchup bottling factory that had advertised for positions. Shimon was hired immediately. He was assured that he would not have to work on *Shabbos* and would be allowed to make up the hours from Monday to Friday. The pay was seven-fifty for a sixty-hour week, and Shimon was pleased to do specific work and earn a set salary for it.

# CHAPTER 13

★

While Shimon's life was settling into a routine, the world around him was slipping into chaos. For Faige in Skalat, the war deepened her already severe difficulties immeasurably. She was in the last months of her pregnancy and had to care for Kalman and operate the grain store on her own.

Like Shimon, many of Skalat's men had emigrated, while others were conscripted into the army. With nearly everyone's situation strained, Faige found no one to help her. To make matters worse, Zvi Hersh had grown gradually apathetic to her situation. Faige and her father-in-law had never gotten along very well, both of them possessing strong wills and the boldness to express them. But now, Zvi Hersh seemed to ignore her completely.

As the war in Europe became a reality, Zvi Hersh thought that his son Shimon, like so many other men forced to separate from their wives and children, would eventually abandon his family. Subconsciously, he felt responsible for initiating Shimon's departure and vented his guilt and vexation on Faige.

On May 28, just before the outbreak of World War I, Faige gave birth to a baby girl. She was named Neshe, after Shimon's mother. But the happiness of her birth was quickly overshadowed by the impending war.

Almost as soon as the war broke out, Faige discovered that running the grain store had become a perilous business. Faige's business relationship with Ivan Padonsky remained firm, but it was now dangerous to travel to his mill for the grain, since the war zone between Austria and Russia ran through the outskirts of Skalat. Out of desperation, however, Faige continued her commute.

Hard times had come to the people of Skalat. Economic activity had ceased, and a hard currency all but vanished. Faige was in dire straits. Despite her hazardous efforts at selling grain, she still did not have enough money to feed her family.

Faige had one onerous choice left. She shed her pride and knocked on her father-in-law's door.

"Herr Halevy," Faige began as she approached him. "I am only coming to you now for help because I have no one else to turn to."

Zvi Hersh was notably short on sympathy. "It is very difficult for many women whose husbands have abandoned their families."

"But you of all people know that it was not Shimon's choice to leave. It was your idea. He had to go to America to stay alive."

Zvi Hersh ignored her accusation. "I didn't cause the quarrels and enemies that Shimon made, nor did I cause this war."

"Herr Halevy, you are my children's grandfather," Faige said indignantly. "You have a responsibility to them, if not to me. If you refuse to help, I will stand in the middle of the street during the next market day and announce to everyone that Zvi Hersh refuses to help his grandchildren."

Zvi Hersh was incredulous, but he knew the threat to his reputation was real.

"I do believe that you would do that," he said, incensed. "You *would* embarrass me in such a way. I'll help you if I have to, but I'll never forgive you for the lack of respect that you've shown me."

It had been a test of wills, and Faige had won. Zvi Hersh began to allot a weekly stipend to Faige, which she used to help pay for the ever increasing price of grain from Padonsky. But that money was still not enough.

Faige was forced to implement an ambitious but dangerous plan. Twice a week, she crossed the no-man's land of war to the neighboring Russian towns, who were in desperate need of grain. Because she could charge higher prices on the Russian border, Faige was able to afford higher prices for the grain, thus insuring a steady supply even in wartime. Her life was in constant danger, but she made enough to support herself and her children.

Faige made another decision. Every Friday she gave grain to bake *challah* free of charge to any woman whose husband was either in the army or in America. Faige felt that there was no surer way to feel Shimon's presence than to give away grain to needy people.

She also wrote a letter to Shimon, telling him of Neshe's birth. She restricted the letter to the bare facts, afraid of the emotions that might drench the message. It was the last letter that Shimon received from Faige for five years.

When Shimon received the letter, he was at the Gross's house in Jersey City. His eyes widened in astonishment as he read its contents.

"Faige had a baby? I can't believe it!" he shouted.

"*Mazel tov*, Shimon!" Tante Frieda exclaimed. "Now you have a wife and *two* children in Skalat."

Shimon was overwrought. "Can you imagine what I did by coming to America? I left a pregnant wife and a one-year-old son on their own. Here I am in safety, while Faige is in the midst of a war zone with two children."

Shimon folded the letter and hung his head in remorse. "I have to do something," he said.

"What do you propose to do?" asked Jacob, who had accompanied him to Jersey City.

"I am going to go back to Skalat," Shimon replied with determination.

"There is no going back now," Jacob said. "The United States is neutral in the war, and they're not allowing any passenger ships to Europe until the war is over."

"Then I will enlist in the United States Army and ask them to send me to Europe."

"You're being ridiculous, Shimon," Jacob said impatiently. "Why should this country accept you in the army? What country would they send you to if they're neutral?"

"I don't know, but I'm going to find out," Shimon insisted.

The next day at the ketchup factory, Shimon used an interpreter to ask his foreman for some time off. The foreman, a huge, good-natured Swede named Nelsen, was often amused by the immigrant workers he dealt with.

"Where do you have to go, Shimon?" Nelson asked.

"I want to enlist in the United States Army."

"You what! Why would you want to do that?"

"I have to get to Europe, Mr. Nelson," Shimon explained. "Enlisting in the army is the only way for me to get back home."

Nelsen had to control himself to keep from laughing.

"Take all the time you need, Shimon," he said with a smile. "And if you don't come back, I'll know they took you."

Shimon walked to the Armory on Belmont Avenue and presented himself to the officer seated at the entrance. He made his intentions known through a stream of gestures and the few English words he knew.

Now it was the sergeant's turn to be amused. But he refrained from laughing and led the would-be recruit to a table with application forms. He motioned to a clerk to assist him. Shimon passed a physical, filled out myriad forms and was finally ushered into an office for disposition.

"Mr. Halevy, I think it's very nice of you to want to enlist in the army," the officer began. "But we cannot accept you. You are not a citizen of this country, and you are overage. Our recruits are usually eighteen years old, and you are twenty-eight. If you were a citizen, we might be able to accept you because of your prior military experience. However, under the existing circumstances, there is no way you can be inducted into the army."

Shimon was deeply disappointed and anguished over the fact that he could do nothing to help Faige. He left the Armory with the rejected application folded in his pocket and returned to the factory to finish the day's work.

A few weeks later, however, an opportunity presented itself to provide Faige with some assistance. Someone had located a Jewish merchant marine, who was leaving on a cargo ship headed for England. The man had offered to mail letters to anywhere in Europe.

"That's wonderful," Shimon said to Yosef and Mordechai, seeing an opportunity to send Faige some money. "But how do we know we can trust him?"

"What difference does that make?" Yosef answered. "It's a chance. The only thing we can lose is money, and we might be able to get a message to our wives."

The three resolved to give the man fifty dollars each to mail to their wives and an additional thirty dollars as payment for his efforts.

Shimon was at a loss. He didn't have the sixty dollars he

needed and felt the venture was too chancy to enlist Jacob's aid. Mordechai and Yosef decided to give Shimon thirty dollars each. Shimon was extremely grateful. He did not want to incur the loan but felt he had no choice for Faige's sake. He resolved to repay the debts, knowing his salary at the ketchup factory was barely enough for him to live on.

He had an idea. There was an Italian named Tony who came to Prince Street every Sunday looking for day laborers to help him with his ice business. Tony picked up his ice in huge blocks at a factory near Mulberry Street and needed help to transport and cut them into manageable sizes.

Shimon had worked with Tony on a previous Sunday but had barely gotten through the day because of the extreme cold and weight of the ice. Still, the pay of four dollars per day was substantial. Shimon resolved to try the job again and give his wages on alternate weeks to Mordechai and Yosef until his loan was paid off. Much that was dear to Shimon remained in Skalat, but his honor travelled with him.

# CHAPTER 14

★

$\mathcal{T}$he war near Skalat continued. Heavy fighting between the Austro-German forces and the Russian army shattered the peace of the small town.

Years after the war, Kalman was able to recall looking through a hole in the hastily constructed fence in the rear of his house. He remembered seeing the opposing Russian and German cavalries ride toward each other and feeling his mother snatch him away from the view.

"This is not for you to see," Faige told him. "Get back into the house."

Faige provided little protection for herself, however. She continued to drive her horse and wagon twice a week through the battlefield to the Russian border cities to sell grain.

Her brother Eli thought that she was committing suicide and told her so.

"I try to pick a day when there is a lull in the fighting," Faige explained. "Then all I have to be afraid of is the long-distance shelling, which isn't very accurate."

Eli was alarmed. "The shelling doesn't have to be accurate to hit you."

Faige knew Eli was right. She could easily be killed on one of her rides, but she refused to accept a life of privation for her children. She also had an innate optimism about her situation that kept her going. Despite her travails, Faige believed that she would not be killed, that the war would end, and that Shimon would return to her.

Faige's predicament worsened before it got better. After *Rosh Hashanah* of 1917, both Kalman and Neshe developed the measles. Kalman rapidly recovered, but two-and-a-half-year-old Neshe did not. For five days and nights Faige cuddled the little girl in her arms, while she applied cold compresses to her body. Nothing helped ease the little girl's discomfort. Moments after a cold bath, Faige felt Neshe's body temperature rising again as she dried her.

Faige held the child in her arms and softly hummed Yiddish lullabies. They alone seemed to soothe the child's distress and her own. Faige was too numb to think, but a cascade of emotions rushed through her. Neshe was going to die without ever having known her father.

Shortly after noon two days before *Sukkos*, Faige knew that she was holding a lifeless form in her arms. She did not cry but simply placed Neshe in her bed. She went to the front door of the house and asked a passerby to summon the rabbi. Neshe was buried the following day.

After *Yom Tov*, the fifty-dollar money order Shimon had sent almost a year before finally arrived. Faige broke down completely. The woman who had held together through the trauma of three years of loneliness, war and the death of her daughter couldn't cope with the strange, proxied reappearance of her husband.

After a time, Faige somewhat recovered and resumed her business and travels. To Faige's surprise, her merchandising talents began to pay off, as she cultivated a welcoming clientele in both Skalat and the Russian border towns. She was actually becoming wealthy. The thickening drawers in her dresser were soon bulging with the piling monies. Faige had diversified as well, hoarding an array of different national currencies as a hedge against the eventual winner of the war, whoever it might be.

She resolved not to reveal her new wealth to anyone and fantasized showing Shimon the money when he returned home. Zvi Hersh, meanwhile, continued to give his daughter-in-law her weekly allowance, as per his reluctant agreement.

On one of her visits to her father-in-law, the newly affluent Faige enjoyed what she thought was an invisible smile as she accepted his unnecessary payment. But Zvi Hersh's lifetime of experience in the business world allowed him to suspect the truth.

"I am wondering, Faige," he said, "if you still require this help that I give you."

"I'm surprised you would ask such a question," Faige retorted. "You know the amount of money it takes to exist these days."

"I don't really care if you need the money or not," Zvi Hersh answered curtly. "I promised you help, and I always keep my word."

Faige was thankful for the money she had accumulated, because as the war progressed, she began to feel more endangered travelling to the Russian towns. Until now, she had relied on protection from the Czar's armies who controlled the border area and generally sanctioned her selling activities. Now, however, that same area could be ruled alternately by Germans, or White, Red or Czarist Russians.

Faige decided to halt her trips to the border temporarily.

Her decision was reinforced when, on July 16, 1918, the deposed Russian Czar Nicholas II and his family were executed by orders of the Ural regional council.

Faige heard the news from Padonsky on one of her trips to the mill.

"How can citizens of a country murder their Czar?" she asked in amazement.

"They will not get away with it easily," Padonsky assured her. "The British have landed an army at Vladivostok, and the United States and Russia have severed relations with each other. Now, no one can predict how the Russian Revolution will be resolved. But you can take my word for it, Faige, the war is almost over."

"I don't see how you can say that in the midst of all these battles," Faige said disbelievingly.

"The signs are all around you. Germany and Austria have sent a note to the United States asking for an armistice. The latest report revealed that the Central Powers have agreed to accept President Wilson's peace terms. That has to mean the end of the war."

Padonsky's prediction proved to be correct. By November of 1918, Kaiser Wilhelm II resigned, and the People's Delegates assumed power in Germany. In December, a triumphant President Wilson arrived in Paris for the Peace Conference that would formally end World War I.

When the war was finally over, the joyous news spread like wildfire through the ketchup factory in Newark. For the first time ever, the assembly line rolled along unattended. Workers hugged each other, laughed, cried, shouted and screamed. Bottles of beer suddenly appeared, and the workers fought to get a bottle.

After it became obvious that no more work would be done, the manager announced a plant holiday for the remainder of the day, assuring the workers they would receive their normal pay.

The walk from the plant to Lustbader's typically took Shimon ten minutes. That day, it took Shimon over an hour. Crowds were everywhere, dancing and singing, and parades jaunted through the multitudes.

Shimon was elated. He finally would be allowed to go home. The following Monday, Shimon, Mordechai and Yosef went to the passport office in New York. The lines to the office stretched for ten blocks into the streets.

Before taking a place in line, the three approached a man from the passport office.

"Is this the line for passports and visas?" Shimon asked.

"That depends where you want to go," the man answered.

"We want to go to Skalat, Austria," Yosef said.

"There's no chance of going to Austria yet. The Russians are in the middle of a revolution over there, and the State Department hasn't lifted the restrictions on Eastern European travel. It's too early."

Shimon moaned in disappointment, and the three friends headed back to Lustbader's. Yosef was silent during the walk.

"What are you thinking about?" Mordechai asked him.

"I'm wondering whether not being able to return to Skalat is such a bad thing. If I go back now, my wife and I will probably renew our old debate of where we should settle, and I don't want to give her a choice. Things are really going well for me in America."

Shimon was horrified. "Don't tell me you're going to abandon your wife?"

"Of course not," Yosef answered. "When the restrictions are lifted and we're allowed to travel, I intend to send her a thousand-dollar money order. With that amount of money, she could come first class if she wants to."

"A thousand dollars," Shimon mused. "That's a lot of money you've earned. I haven't been able to save anything."

"Well, Shimon, you earn seven-fifty a week," Yosef said. "I've been making fifty dollars a week and more on my own cans of tuna fish. I'm in the process of renting two stores here on Prince Street to start my own warehouse. The canning company has agreed to put my label on the tuna fish, so I'll be advertising my own business. It's going to be called Yosef brand tuna fish."

"Wow, that's big news, Yosef," Shimon exclaimed. "I had no idea things were advancing for you that fast. I'm still worried about how to get enough money to return to Skalat."

Yosef smiled at Shimon. "I've thought of that, and I know how hard it is for you to go to your brother for money. I'd like to give or loan you three hundred dollars to get you back to Skalat."

"How can I thank you?" Shimon said as tears spilled from his eyes. "I only hope it won't take me too long to repay you."

Shimon turned to Mordechai. "How about you, Mordechai? Will you be coming along?"

"Yes, but I don't intend to stay in Skalat any more than I have to," Mordechai answered. "I'm going to bring my wife and son back here with me. I'm not doing as well as Yosef, but I've been making fifteen dollars a week as a *shochet*, and I've been offered a position as a *chazan* in a new *shul* starting up on Kinney Street. I really like America. I couldn't live in Skalat any more."

"Well," Shimon said slowly, "I guess I'm the only one who will be staying there. I also like America, but I can't continue to disrupt my family's lives, especially after what they've gone through in the war."

# CHAPTER 15

★

*I*n Skalat, Faige also heard talks of peace but continued to see only war. The empires of Turkey and Austria-Hungary were gone, replaced by the threatening nationalism of the peoples left behind.

Women in Skalat, whose husbands had fled to America, began to receive letters from them. Faige waited patiently to hear from Shimon, but months passed without any word. Faige began to worry.

"Perhaps, Faige," her sister Sarah told her, "you ought to recognize the possibility that Shimon does not intend to return to you."

Faige got angry.

"I don't see how you can say that," she said. "You only have to look around to convince yourself that there is still plenty of fighting going on."

Faige was excusing Shimon as much to herself as to her sister.

"But there is an armistice," Sarah said. "It's possible to send letters again. From what I see, many men are not going to come home. America must be every bit as good as they say."

When Sarah left, Faige sat down to write to Shimon. She had sensed the logic in Sarah's words and feared waiting to hear the truth any longer.

Dear Shimon,

I hope that you are well. This is the first letter you have received since I told you of my pregnancy so many years ago. We had a beautiful, blond-haired, blue-eyed girl whom I called Neshe. She died on *Sukkos* 1917, when she was two-and-a-half years old. It's tragic that you never knew her. She and Kalman both got the measles. He recovered; she did not.

The war is and was as horrible as you can imagine. Thank Heaven we survived. Kalman and I are both fine. About Kalman, he was six years old this past September. Kalman is tall and very good-looking. He is in the Halevy tradition, but mostly Kalman is just very good. He is easy to bring up and a pleasure to be with.

I know you did the right thing by going to America, but now people are receiving and sending letters. I don't know how you managed to send me the fifty dollars, but the most important part was that you still remembered your wife.

In conclusion, I want to tell you that if there is no writing paper to be found in America, get word to me and I'll send you some.

Love, Faige

Shimon was devastated upon reading of the death of his daughter whom he had never seen. He also felt guilty at not having thought of writing to Faige to let her know of his plans. Mordechai was with Shimon when he read Faige's letter.

"I have been so excited about the prospect of going back

that I forgot I could write to her," Shimon told Mordechai. "Will you help me write the letter?"

"Of course," was the expected reply, "I always believe in helping a man communicate with his wife."

# CHAPTER 16

★

*I*t was not until 1920 that the State Department finally allowed travel to Eastern Europe. Shimon and Mordechai left the United States immediately after *Pesach* of 1920.

Despite his excitement at returning to Skalat, Shimon was sad to leave his home in America. The Morton Street Shul held a lavish *kiddush* commemorating his departure for home, and Shimon was touched by the number of friends he had made there.

At the ketchup factory, Nelsen blew the whistle that ordered the halting of the production belt. Immediately, cans of beer and sandwiches were set up in the factory for a good-bye party for Shimon. Nelsen also presented Shimon with a billfold that contained ten dollars, a present collected from his co-workers.

The Grosses held a farewell dinner, too, at Tante Frieda's house. Martin gave Shimon a package for his trip, containing several long salamis, a bolonga, breads, mustard and two bottles of whiskey. Shimon hesitated over the whiskey, knowing that

Prohibition was still technically in force, but he was assured that no one would comb his personal belongings.

Parting from Jacob was the most difficult. Jacob drove Shimon and Mordechai to New York on the day they left. The brot͘ ers were composed up until Shimon was ready to board the ship. Then they broke down.

'What's most painful is that we'll probably never see each other again," Jacob said, wiping away his tears.

"I know, Jacob, but I suppose this is the way it has to be. I have to go back."

"Please send my regards to the family, though they probably have forgotten me by now," Jacob said. "Tell them that if anyone ever wants to come to America, I would be happy to help."

He paused and looked silently at Shimon before continuing. "I still think you're making a mistake by not wanting to come back to America, but if you change your mind for any reason, just write. I brought you over once, and I wouldn't hesitate to do it again."

Shimon thanked Jacob, and they exchanged final good-byes. Then Shimon and Mordechai walked up the planks to board the ship. The scene was a good deal more orderly than their voyage to America seven years before, with a notable demographic change. Few families were making the trip. Almost all were men.

A crewman with a megaphone instructed the passengers where to go. "Step lively, please. This ship is not completely full, and there are not many first-class passengers. You can take any empty cabin you find."

"Did you hear that, Mordechai?" Shimon shouted. "Let's hurry to the upper deck. Maybe we'll be lucky and make the trip in style."

The men were indeed very fortunate, managing to claim a

well-situated cabin on the third deck.

"Our friends should see us now," Shimon said with a laugh. "After seven years in America, we're going home like millionaires."

Three weeks later, the boat docked in Belgium. After disembarking, they took a train to Berlin and then a second train to Lemberg.

"Do you remember that it was here that we met for the first time?" Shimon recalled when they reached Lemberg.

"Like it was yesterday," Mordechai replied. "But I didn't think we would be gone this long. Do we walk or try to get a ride to Skalat?"

"It's only two miles," Shimon said. "Let's run."

The two friends raced to Skalat and stood at the outskirts of the town's streets. A rush of memories swept over Shimon, and his eyes grew moist as he surveyed the quiet scene around him.

"Seven years is a long time," he observed in almost a whisper.

Mordechai turned to Shimon. "I'll never forget you, Shimon. You are truly one of the best friends a man can have."

"And so are you," Shimon replied. "Please look me up before you go back to America."

The two friends hugged each other and separated.

# CHAPTER 17

★

*S*himon was now alone on the main street of Skalat. He began to walk nervously toward his grain store. Shmuel Hakatan, Shimon's life-long friend, recognized him first.

"Shimon, it's you!" a stupefied Shmuel cried. "You're back in Skalat! What happened to your beard and your long coat? I can't believe it!"

Shimon's clothes were once again an anomaly. Considering his appearance, Shimon was surprised Shmuel had recognized him at all. The men started to hug each other when Shmuel suddenly pulled away.

"Wait," he explained. "Your son is right here."

Shmuel motioned to a group of youngsters playing nearby. He approached the tallest and pulled him away.

"Kalman," he told the boy, "this is your father."

Shimon and Kalman looked at each other in a long silence. Both started to cry as Shimon held him tight. Finally, Kalman grabbed his father's hand and started to pull him forward.

"Come," he said, "we have to go to Mamme."

Kalman pulled his father through the streets with an ec-static urgency. They stormed through the door of the store and found Faige sorting out bags of grain behind the counter. When she looked up to see the two, she let out a shriek and dropped a bag of grain with a thud.

Faige stared at her husband, unable to move. She was petri-fied into silence with the weight of seven years' suffering and the fear of never seeing her husband again.

Finally, she managed to speak. "Shimon . . . you are really here . . . you are home! I don't believe it! Do you know how much I prayed for this moment? Thank you, dear Lord, for returning my husband to me!"

"You see," Shimon stammered, "if you live long enough, you see miracles."

"It's a miracle that you see us, too, after this war," Faige said between tears.

She looked closely at Shimon. "What did you do to your beard? And you of all people in a short jacket?"

"The American influence," Shimon responded with a sheep-ish smile.

The two did not have much time to speak after that. The news of Shimon's return spread quickly through the town, and waves of guests came to welcome Shimon home. Zvi Hersh and Zipporah, the Halevy sisters and their families, the rabbis and Shimon's friends all came to see the beloved returnee. Shimon was overwhelmed by their genuine warmth and sincerity.

"In Newark," he told Faige after they had all left, "the only relative I had was Jacob. I had Tante Frieda, but she lives with her children in Jersey City. In sheer numbers, I had nothing similar to what I saw tonight."

"That is the main reason why I would never go to America," Faige said. "Why should I leave everything and everybody I have been accustomed to all my life to become a stranger somewhere else?"

"America is not like anywhere else," Shimon said. But he didn't try to explain, because he knew he could never describe America to Faige or anyone else who had never been there.

Shimon was in Skalat only one day, and already he began comparing it to the towns of America. Newark and Skalat, he thought to himself, what a study in contrasts! Newark is big, Skalat is small; Newark is boisterous and frenetic, Skalat is subdued and immured in routine; Newark is filled with opportunities, while Skalat is filled with almost none. Shimon pondered the differences but hesitated to share them with Faige. Was he mistaken to have come back?

Faige quickly shook Shimon out of his reverie.

"Shimon," she began, approaching him, "have you noticed anything unusual in our furniture drawers?"

"What a strange question," Shimon replied, advancing to his dresser and tugging at the first drawer.

Shimon was shocked at what he saw. "Where did this money come from?"

"Some came from store profits," Faige answered proudly, "but most came from my trips to the Russian border towns to sell grain."

Shimon was incredulous. "What! You travelled to the Russian towns during the war? You risked your life for money?"

"I had to," Faige answered, "to avoid relying on *tzeddakah*. Your father helped us a little, but what he gave us wasn't nearly enough to live on."

"But what about the store?"

"The store didn't sell enough to sustain us. The Russians desperately needed the grain I sold them. It was risky, but it worked. I stopped going there only a few months ago, because it got too dangerous."

"How much money is here?" Shimon asked hesitantly.

"I don't know. When I saw how much money was accumulating, I didn't know what to do with it and just kept stuffing it into the drawers. I never counted it."

During the following months, Faige's seeing eyes told her the money was thinning in the drawers. But she didn't care. It was wonderful to have Shimon home. The mere sight of her husband doing ordinary things thrilled her. Once again, they were a family. Shimon began working at the grain store. He was well-liked by the townspeople, and the ambience of the store reflected his relaxed bearing. Faige maintained the job of buying grain, trusting herself to deal better with Padonsky than Shimon.

But even with Faige's involvement, the store began to show less and less profit. An aggravated Faige knew why.

"Shimon, I think we're having the same problem in the store we had before you left," she said.

"What do you mean?" Shimon asked.

"What do I mean? I mean you are not charging the prices we agreed upon. Look at our account book."

"But look how many customers come to us," Shimon said, trying to defend his performance.

"Sure, our store is popular," Faige said. "People love to come here and talk about everything under the sun, but when they leave they don't pay."

"That's not completely true," Shimon answered in partial rebuttal. "I try to charge the correct amount in most cases and use my judgment in the others."

"What others?" Faige practically shrieked. "To what others are you referring?"

"The poor, the sick, the widows," Shimon answered, raising his voice in turn. "I can't charge them the same prices as everyone else."

"But don't you see what is happening?" Faige said in an exasperated tone. "People are not fools. Once they know our prices depend upon their ability to pay, they send the sickest member of the family to do the shopping. It's getting to the point where I can see the disappointment on a customer's face if I am the one who takes care of him. That's the price of your popularity, Shimon. You take money out of our pocket and put it in theirs. I've noticed how the money is going down in our chest drawers. We can't stay in business this way."

Faige started to put on her overcoat.

"Where are you going?" Shimon asked.

"I'm so upset I'm going to Padonsky for another order of grain. Maybe the ride will calm me down."

"Wait, I'll harness the horse and wagon for you," Shimon offered, but the olive branch was quickly snapped.

"You don't have to, Shimon. I managed for seven years without you. I can still do it myself."

Faige wasn't gone ten minutes when Shimon heard her desperate cries for help. "Shimon, come quickly! I'm bleeding terribly!"

Shimon rushed outside and found Faige lying on the ground beside the horse and wagon. Blood was shooting out of a deep, ugly wound on her right thigh.

Shimon instructed Faige to be still and asked a passerby to summon Dr. Kromm. Then he ran back into the house and brought out towels to cover the wound. But they failed to stop the bleeding, absorbing horrific red blots as soon as they were applied. Dr. Kromm arrived just as Shimon was placing the last towel on Faige's leg.

"These towels will not do," he said. "Get me a clean sheet and a pair of scissors."

Dr. Kromm cut a long strip out of the sheet about four inches wide, asked Shimon to prepare several similar-sized shards and started to dress the wound. After applying five tightly-cinched strips, he at last capped the geyser of blood.

"This is a nasty cut," Dr. Kromm said. "How did you get it?"

Faige was so weak she could barely answer. Shimon walked over to the wagon.

"Look at this," he said, pointing to the step used to climb onto the wagon. A large, rusty nail jutted out from its side.

"I can't believe I never noticed it before," Shimon said guiltily. "Is she hurt badly?"

"From the looks of that nail, we do have to worry about blood poisoning," Dr. Kromm answered. "In the meantime, let's get her to bed."

Dr. Kromm attended to Faige in the house and closed the door behind him before addressing Shimon.

"I think the dressing has stopped the bleeding," he said, "but I have to clean it as soon as possible. I don't like the looks of that nail. I'm going to my home to get some supplies, and I'll be right back. In the meantime, don't let Faige get out of bed until we know what we are dealing with."

When Dr. Kromm returned, his assessment of Faige's predicament was more grim.

"I cleaned up the wound as best as I could, but she almost certainly has an infection there," he told Shimon.

"Is it serious?" Shimon looked alarmed. "She is pregnant, you know."

"Faige has a slight temperature now," Dr. Kromm said. "We'll have to see if it drops in the next couple of days. I want her to get a lot of bed rest and make sure she takes three hot baths a day, as hot as she can stand it. We have to make sure we try to get rid of that infection. A long-lasting infection could be serious for her and the baby she is carrying."

# CHAPTER 18

★

"A danger to the baby . . ." Shimon repeated, almost in a daze. "A danger to the baby."

"Right now the wound doesn't look so bad," Dr. Kromm reassured him, "but we have to watch it closely. If an infection develops in the next few days, and I think one will, the wound will redden and turn pussy. The ulcer can easily conduct poison into the bloodstream. That is why the baby will almost certainly be affected. The longer it takes for Faige's body to fight off the infection, the worse it will be for the baby."

Over the next few days, the ulcer did indeed redden and widen. Faige was not told of the probable infection of the baby. She carefully observed all the doctor's instructions, while tending to most of her duties in the house and in the store. But she suffered almost constant pain.

Shimon took her to Lemberg and Tarnapol in the hope that the doctors there would be able to hasten a cure. The doctors of both cities upheld Dr. Kromm's diagnosis, but for the most part they could do little to augment her treatment.

By the spring of 1921, about five months after the accident occurred, the ulcer stopped oozing, lost much of its fearsome redness and began to shrink. By the sixth month, Dr. Kromm felt that Faige was cured. She was delighted, while Shimon and the doctor remained silently apprehensive.

During Faige's recuperation, the grain store began suffering serious setbacks. Shimon tried to curb his attempts at charity, but problems arose elsewhere. On one of his trips to the mill, Shimon was told that his next purchase would cost double the present amount.

"You shouldn't take it personally," Padonsky explained. "Inflation is rising badly in Europe. We depend on the German mark for stability, and it's been falling rapidly because they've been forced to pay reparations."

It took Shimon three days to tell Faige about the increase.

"This is terrible. It will cripple our business," she lamented.

Throughout the summer, though they had the money in the drawer to rely on, Shimon and Faige grew increasingly apprehensive about their situation. Then, to make matters worse, Shimon lost three thousand dollars of their savings in a bad investment deal with a lumber yard. He had invested the money with the reluctant approval of Faige, and now he was devastated at its loss.

On July 27, their troubled situation was cheered by the birth of a baby boy. From observation and the physical examination at birth, the baby looked normal.

"I'm amazed," Dr. Kromm said. "Everything tells me that there has to be something wrong with the baby. Faige had the infection going through her body for five to six months, and yet I can't see anything wrong. We'll have to keep a close watch on him. There must be something I am missing."

The baby was named Reuven Joshua Halevy, in memory of

Shimon's sister's husband, who had died not long before. Shimon and Faige called him Joshua.

Dr. Kromm's suspicions about Joshua's health were confirmed. Four months after his *bris,* Joshua spent a restless night, coughing, refusing his feeding and running a temperature. At daybreak, Shimon went to fetch the doctor.

"This is the ailment that was not picked up before," Dr. Kromm said, after examining the baby. "Joshua has congenital heart disease."

"What does that mean?" Faige asked anxiously.

"Well," answered Dr. Kromm, "there are several different types, and we don't know which one Joshua has. He will most likely always have it. Heart disease is a long-range diagnosis. Right now Joshua has double pneumonia, and we have to cure that immediately."

Shimon gasped. "And we thought we had gotten away with nothing."

"In a sense you did," Doctor Kromm answered. "If I were to tell you about all the terrible things that could have happened, you might be willing to accept this problem happily. Joshua will be all right. He looked pretty healthy before the pneumonia, and we ought to be able to take care of that."

Joshua suffered for almost two weeks before the pneumonia cleared up. The rest of that summer, Shimon and Faige were busy improving the store. Wholesale prices for their grain had doubled, and they had difficulty making payments for it.

More and more, Shimon began thinking of going back to America with his family. He could not compare the opportunities there with what was available in Skalat. He tried telling Faige of how happy he had been at his job in the ketchup factory. He watched somewhat enviously as his friend Mordechai set off for America with his wife and son. Yosef's wife had left long before when she received the money order for a thousand dollars.

Faige heard Shimon's arguments, but she refused to consider going to America—until one *Shabbos* towards the end of the summer.

That *Shabbos* Skalat was the scene of a Ukrainian raid. The attack was interpreted as part of the struggle between Russia and Poland over disputed border territory and was particularly vicious. The riders came in on their huge horses with long swords swinging at their side, killing anyone they saw.

Fortunately, they struck in the late afternoon, before the men had returned to *shul*. The timing thus saved many lives, as whole families were able to hide quickly.

Shimon hid his family in the house and listened to the noises outside. From the sounds in the street, Shimon knew the Cossacks were in front of his grain store. He listened as the men ransacked the contents of the shelves. They poured the merchandise into huge sacks, which they seemed to have readied for just such purposes. After hoarding all the grain, the Cossacks turned their swords to the shelves, sundering them to pieces.

Shimon remained under his bed, shaking with fury. Had he been alone, he would have charged the pillagers in the hope of killing some before being killed. But his wife and children were hidden in the loft, and the idea seemed foolhardy, even selfish.

After they had ravaged the store, two Cossacks entered the house. They were inches away from Shimon, who was now hiding under the bed, and he watched as they dredged the drawers with rapacious glee. When they saw the money squirreled in them, they squealed with delight. In an almost drunken frenzy they danced into the street, battling crazily over their booty.

Their waning shouts told Shimon the attack was over, and the Halevy family slowly emerged from their shelter. Shimon came out from under the bed shuddering, his eyes almost ablaze.

"Shimon, what's the matter with you?" Faige said. "You act

as if you have never lived through a pogrom before."

"Faige, don't you see how unfair this is? You worked hard, risked your life to get some money together and now overnight it's all gone. How is it possible to live this way?"

"Look at it this way," Faige responded implacably. "We should be happy that we all survived the raid. It could have been worse."

"Well, it doesn't have to be like this, Faige," Shimon answered emphatically. "I've seen another way. This couldn't have happened in America. I had forgotten how it is to live under continual fear. Here, you have to worry about the *goyim* even without pogroms. They kill and rob whomever they want, and no one does anything about it."

Faige tried to calm her outraged husband.

"Shimon, we'll start anew as we always do," she said. "You'll repair the store as best as you can. I'll go to the mill. I'm sure Mr. Padonsky will give us merchandise on credit. He knows what has happened to us. We'll be all right."

Shimon didn't look convinced. The rest of that *Shabbos* he was depressed and sullen. The following day, he set out to clean up the grain store. As he was closing the door behind him, he suddenly ran back in.

"Where is Kalman?" he asked Faige in alarm.

"Kalman?" Faige repeated. The abruptness of Shimon's question took Faige by surprise. "He is with his cousin Velvel. There is no *cheder* today because of the raid, and Kalman went there to see if he could help Chana and the children straighten up."

Shimon looked crestfallen. "That's terrible," he said as he bolted towards the door.

"Why?" Faige asked nervously.

"Because the Cossacks didn't leave yet, and it's rumored they're not going to leave. They're setting up a permanent army camp on the outskirts of Skalat, right near Chana's house. They're grabbing anyone they can, mostly Jews, to build their camp."

"You mean they would draft a nine-year-old boy into the army?" Faige gasped.

"I mean just that," Shimon answered as he barreled through the door.

Shimon ran the two miles to Chana's house, but as he approached the Russian camp, instinct led him off the street. He walked the rest of the way through the undergrowth and woods that paralleled the main road.

As he reached the outskirts of Chana's house, he saw a short, heavyset Cossack dragging two boys toward the camp. They were Kalman and Velvel.

"What a find," the Cossack said in a drunken slur. "The captain will be very pleased to let you help us build the platform for the camp. Maybe the captain will like you enough to allow you to join the army, like they do in Russia. Wouldn't you like that?"

The Cossack started laughing uproariously. Shimon made an instant decision. Brandishing a large limb he had scavenged in the woods, he jumped in front of the startled Cossack and struck him across his face and head. As the Cossack fell, Shimon bolted on top of him and pulled out the soldier's knife. He plunged the knife repeatedly into his chest, aiming where he thought the Cossack's heart was.

He shouted at the startled boys. "Run quickly! Get out of here and go to our house! Kalman, tell Mamme to stay home. I'll be there soon."

Shimon dragged the man's body into the woods, left the knife in the corpse and wiped the blood from his hands in the leaves and grass. Then he cut back to the main road to avoid being found in the woods with the body. Almost as soon as

Shimon reached the road, he saw two Cossacks walking toward him.

"Look what we have here," one said as he approached Shimon. "It's a Jew who I am sure would like to volunteer a day's work on our campsite."

As the Cossacks dragged Shimon away, Kalman and Velvel reached home. Their return without their rescuer gave Faige reason to fear for Shimon's life. Faige went to the barren store and kept a frantic vigil for her husband. Toward the mid-afternoon, her brother Eli reported that he had seen Shimon working on the Ukrainian platform. Faige exhaled a sigh of relief. At least he was still alive.

After dark, a bedraggled Shimon finally came home. Faige gasped when she saw him. His clothes were almost completely torn from his body, and mud and sweat had hardened on his face and limbs. He was coatless and bareheaded, and the slits in his shirt and torn pants divulged bloody cuts, bruises and scrapes. His face was contorted in pain and indignation.

After a bath, a good meal and a half-consumed bottle of *schnapps*, Shimon looked somewhat recuperated. When he sat down to talk to Faige, she knew what he had in mind.

"Faige," Shimon began, "I don't think I can take any more of this. Nothing is going right for us. The business, for one thing, has to be started all over again."

"That's not my fault," Faige quickly countered. "I had a successful business before you came home."

"That's not the point. If I hadn't lost the money in the lumber yard deal, the Ukrainians would certainly have stolen it in the raid. And even if we do build up our grain store again, who's to say that our money won't be stolen in another raid? It's impossible to live here. You have never seen any other place, and you think that things have to be this way forever. They don't."

"What are you suggesting?" Faige asked, though she already knew.

"I'm suggesting that we go to America. I think it's the only place for us to live now. You would love America, Faige. People are free there. There are so many opportunities there."

Faige didn't say anything, and Shimon took that as a sign to continue. "Just look at Jacob, Faige. He's becoming wealthy. He will be in business for himself shortly. He drives a car and isn't afraid of someone taking it away from him. The man I told you about, Yosef Kagan, he's in his own business already. Look, Faige, I tried. I didn't intend to ask you to go to America. I always said I was going home to stay, but it's just too difficult and too dangerous to live in Skalat, not only for ourselves but for our children. I feel like screaming at the thought of Kalman in the Ukrainian army for the rest of his life."

Shimon slumped back in his chair, his eyes tracing Faige's every movement. He keenly awaited her reaction.

"Well, at least now it's out in the open, Shimon," she began. "I knew someday we would have this talk."

Shimon waited for her to continue, and she did. "I had a feeling you wouldn't want to stay home once you returned. I was hoping that the money I accumulated during the war would make us so comfortable that it would be difficult for you to leave. I don't want to go to America, Shimon. I know America has to be a wonderful place or so many people wouldn't be going there, but I don't want to live in a strange land for the rest of my life. I was born here, and so were you. Our parents, grandparents and their parents have been here for hundreds of years. We know what to expect, the good and the bad. We have no idea what we and our children will have to face in America."

Faige paused and looked at Shimon. "Shimon, I know you've been through a lot today, but we shouldn't make a decision like this because of it. The day is over, you're safe, thank Heaven, and so is Kalman. Why don't we think this over and see what happens?"

The next day, Shimon took advantage of Faige's conciliatory approach to the situation and won her consent to go to Lemberg to inquire about a visa.

It was early afternoon when Shimon reached Lemberg. Once there, Shimon recalled the day nine years earlier when he had gone to Lemberg on the same mission. What a difference, he thought. In 1913, there had been crowds of people at the embassy, waiting on line in the hope of gaining visas to take them to America. Now he climbed the steps to the entrance alone.

A solitary marine guard stood watch at the door. "What do you want?" he demanded.

"I'd like a visa to go to the United States for me and my family," Shimon answered.

"They are no longer granting visas," came the curt reply. "But I suppose you will want to hear that from an embassy employee. Second door on the right."

A chill went through Shimon's body. Was he too late? He walked down the dark, empty corridor in trepidation. He entered a room and saw a man seated at the desk, buried behind a newspaper. He barely troubled himself to look up from the paper to glance at Shimon.

"What are you here for?" he finally asked.

"I would like a visa to go to the United States," Shimon replied.

The man put down his paper. "Where have you been for the past year?"

"What do you mean?" Shimon asked nervously.

"On May 19, 1921, the United States passed the Emergency Quota Immigration Act. As a result, the quota of immigrants from Poland for 1922 was filled by February. You'll have to wait until next year and try to get on the 1923 list."

"But sir," Shimon interjected, "I have already lived in the United States."

"When did you live there?" the man asked suspiciously.

"From 1913 to 1920," Shimon said excitedly. "I lived in Newark, New Jersey."

"Can you prove that?" the bureaucrat asked.

"Yes, sir," Shimon answered, carefully removing some papers from his pockets. "I tried to enlist in the United States army in 1914 when the war started. Here are the papers they gave me at that time. In 1917, when America entered the war, I registered as an enemy alien according to the law. Here is the card for that."

The man seemed moved by his eagerness. "Did you register your intention to return when you left?" he asked.

"No," Shimon said and then added a rare untruth. "I was not aware I had to do that."

"Well, it would have made it a lot easier for you now had you done so," the man said. "Do you have relatives in the United States who would be able to guarantee you and your family would not become wards of the state?"

"Yes, sir," Shimon answered energetically. "I have a brother in Newark who would be happy to sign any papers you require."

The man finally folded his newspaper. He was impressed with Shimon's sincerity and his papers. Shimon's attempt to enlist in the U.S. army had not been in vain.

"I will try to make out your application as a reentry," he said, allowing himself a smile. "If what you say is true, the papers may be approved. But first I'll have to see if my boss agrees with me."

Two hours later, Shimon left the embassy building with a stack of papers that were his copy of the application to return to the United States. He couldn't believe his good fortune.

The men at the embassy stressed Jacob's affidavit would be

all-important, but Shimon had no doubt it would be forthcoming. He was instructed to return to the embassy a month later for the final decision.

Shimon was flushed with excitement when he returned home. One look at Shimon told Faige that he had been successful.

"Well, when do we leave?" she asked, half in jest.

"September or October," Shimon answered matter-of-factly. "That's if everything goes all right."

He recounted his experience at the American Embassy in careful detail. Then, almost as an afterthought, Shimon turned to his wife.

"Is it settled then? You agree we should go to America?" he asked, hoping the point had already become moot.

"Well, let's say that I have been pushed in that direction by what happened this morning," Faige said. "I went to the mill to try to get some flour on credit so we could reopen the store. Padonsky gave me the grain on credit, but he told me some very disturbing things. For example, he expects the Ukrainian military presence in Skalat to continue indefinitely. Instead of one or two pogroms a year, he feels that we can expect one almost every month. Also, Padonsky doesn't know if he'll be able to continue to give us credit every time we have a raid. The risk is too great."

Shimon looked at his wife, almost enjoying the confirmation of his fears.

"I agree with Padonsky," he said. "The Ukrainians aren't building a permanent camp in Skalat for a short stay."

"It would seem that way," Faige answered rather reluctantly.

Exactly one month after his visit to the American Embassy in Lemberg, Shimon returned there as he had been instructed. The embassy had received papers from Jacob affirming his support of his brother's application. Jacob also indicated he would pay for the shipscards in New York for his brother and his family. Shimon was asked to choose an approximate ship date. He chose a voyage from Belgium three weeks after *Yom Kippur.* It coincided almost exactly with his first departure date.

News of the Halevy plans spread through the Jewish community in Skalat immediately. Even Zvi Hersh endorsed his son's plans, though he knew with certainty that this time he would never see his son again.

# CHAPTER 19

★

*B*efore leaving, Shimon and Faige had to raise money for the trip and for Padonsky, who had been selling them grain for the store on credit.

Shimon decided on a plan. First, he would revisit the lumber yard, where he had lost his investment, and request a job. Second, he instructed Faige to set up a grain outlet alongside her sister Sarah's tavern and sell grain on market days. Finally, Kalman, barely ten years old, was entrusted with the sparsely restocked store, which, along with their house, was set to be handed over to Shimon's widowed sister Chana.

The plan worked. The combined efforts began to pad the family drawers anew with currency. The debt to Padonsky was soon paid off, and the surplus was set aside for travelling fares.

Despite their success, Shimon and Faige could not beat back their persistent apprehensions about their impending trip. Faige was leaving the land of her birth, as she had always dreaded she might. Shimon also realized the enormous responsibility he was undertaking. This time he was not going alone.

The night before their scheduled departure date, Zvi Hersh came to bid them farewell, bringing with him carefully wrapped foods to take with them on their trip.

"I know that you are doing the right thing," Zvi Hersh told Shimon during their final good-byes. "If I were younger, I probably would have gone with you. But I am sixty-seven years old, which is not the age for new adventures."

Zvi Hersh's sadness was mixed with concern. "I'm afraid the Jews will suffer greatly with the coming political changes here. I think you made the right decision to leave, Shimon. I pray you will get to America safely. And tell Jacob, when you see him, that I forgave him a long time ago and wish him well."

Zvi Hersh presented Shimon with a new *tallis*, which had a wide band of silver ornaments threaded into the material. He gave him a similar one to give to Jacob. The two embraced. Then Zvi Hersh kissed the *mezuzah* on the door and left.

The following morning, Shimon went to the *shul* at dawn to *daven* there for the last time. The finality of the event left him with tears in his eyes. When he returned home, Faige's brother Eli drove the family to Lemberg with Shimon's horse and wagon. It was agreed that he would then take possession of them.

Once in Lemberg, Eli wanted to wait until the family boarded the train, but Faige and Shimon insisted he leave. As he drove away, Faige began to cry.

"There goes my wagon," she said. "Do you realize how much I used it while you were gone? I'll never forget those trips I took to the Russian border towns during the war. And remember the nail that gave me that infection?"

Shimon wiped away a tear of his own and went to purchase tickets to Berlin. The train ride to Berlin took twenty-six hours. Despite the length of time in uncomfortable chairs, the family enjoyed the ride immensely. It was the first time Faige and the children had ever ridden on a train.

The railroad station at Berlin was exactly as Shimon had remembered it before the war. It seemed to him, however, that the people were even more hostile than before.

"When we boarded the train in Lemberg," Faige said, "I felt that we looked like a normal family setting out on a trip. Here, I feel odd. It seems as if everybody is staring at us."

"You're right," Shimon answered. "Mordechai and I felt the same way the last time we were here. It seems even worse now."

Shimon and Faige tried to ignore the unfriendly stares of passersby and headed to the ticket counter to purchase tickets to Frankfurt. They chose coach over steerage, because Shimon didn't want to cause his family discomfort.

Frankfurt was not much more welcoming than Berlin. Now, knowing what to expect, Shimon and Faige tried to avoid encounters while seeking out Khal Adath Jeshurun, the Rabbi Samson Raphael Hirsch *shul*. Instead of turning to a policeman, they looked for somebody who appeared Jewish.

Shimon tried to amuse the family with an account of the fight into which he had been drawn during his rescue of Velvel Mandel during his first visit to Frankfurt. Clearly worried about their current circumstances, neither Faige nor Kalman thought it was very funny.

Finally, Faige noticed a man with a short, well-kept beard and a black hat. The man looked at them with obvious, benign interest. Shimon approached him.

"I beg your pardon, sir," Shimon said in faulty German. "Can you please direct me to the Hirsch *shul?*"

"I'll do better than that," the man answered, "I'll take you there. I was going to approach you as soon as I thought it safe. Let's leave the station as quickly as possible. Someone here can start a ruckus at any time for no reason."

In the safety of the *shul*, the family started to relax. The hospitality of the congregants was wondrously unchanged, but the hosts seemed more serious and cautious.

Rabbi Barzel, the benefactor who had retrieved them from the station, explained the mood to Shimon and Faige. "Before the war what happened today occurred regularly. Jews would arrive at the railroad station, we identified them, and we brought them here. There were incidents, but we expected them, and we managed. Today, the mood is more serious. The German people are angry. Their army was defeated in an awful war. And of course, the first people that get blamed are the Jews."

Shimon and Faige decided to stay in Frankfurt over *Shabbos* and the first days of *Sukkos*. When they were ready to go to Belgium, the rabbi of the *shul* advised them to travel by coach.

"It's essential to travel that way for the rest of your trip," he instructed Shimon. "Steerage will be occupied by the poorer Germans, and they are most antagonistic to the Jewish people."

To Shimon's shock and dismay, the total cost of the three tickets in coach was two hundred and ten dollars. At the rate the money was going for tickets and food, Shimon calculated apprehensively that he would only be left with ten dollars by the time he reached the ship.

The trip to Belgium proved to be uneventful. While the family received stares of anger and amusement, they had become accustomed to such behavior and ignored it. Shimon and Faige talked in subdued but happy tones, and Shimon entertained his family with stories of life in America.

Once in Belgium, Shimon spent his last ten dollars to hire a horse and wagon to take him to the Jewish Community Organization. Shimon impressed Faige by giving the driver instructions on how to get there. His knowledge of the route served him well, because as was all too often the case in jittery post-war Europe, no one from the Jewish community waited at the station to greet arrivals.

The Halevys were met enthusiastically at the community center. Some townspeople even remembered Shimon. The greeters explained that their community assistance program for Jews headed to either Palestine or America still operated, but on a somewhat reduced level.

Shimon and Faige were delighted to learn that their ship was due to leave for America the following Tuesday. Among the people at the center that day was the man who had employed Shimon in 1913 to peddle fruits and vegetables. They decided that both Shimon and Kalman would work for him for the few days before the ship left. They were happy to be paid with food, which they could take with them for provisions on the voyage.

The day of their departure finally arrived. The food from Mr. Goldberg did not look to be enough to last the journey, but Shimon and Faige had no choice and decided they would have to make it do. As they took a few steps onto the vessel with their meager possessions, Shimon suddenly gasped. He grabbed Kalman's shoulders and brought him to an immediate halt. There, pinned beneath Kalman's small right shoe, was a twenty-dollar bill. With a surgeon's delicacy, Shimon put his packages down and, slowly lifting up his son's shoe, plucked the bill.

For almost a moment, Shimon and Faige were speechless. The family economy had just been jump-started.

"I'll get you and the children settled somewhere on the ship, and then I'll do some shopping," Shimon said happily.

An hour later, Shimon returned to the steerage deck carrying a large sack of food.

The ocean voyage to America took twenty-six days. As in 1913, entire families lived on the steerage deck, but this time the demographics were different, with the Russian, Polish and Eastern European families a distinct minority.

"The last time I went to America," Shimon told Faige, "The

language of the steerage deck was Yiddish. Now I hardly hear it."

"There may be more *goyim* here," Faige replied, "but I'm not afraid the way I was on the train rides through Europe. It doesn't seem as if the people here resent us. We're all going to the same place."

"Just wait until you reach America," Shimon promised. "You'll feel the same way there."

Faige didn't have much of an opportunity to confirm her assessment of the people on board, because she suffered terrible seasickness and spent the entire trip in the steerage rooms. Shimon took Kalman and Joshua for long walks on the decks. After the first few days they began to greet people on the ship. Shimon also met a kindly steward who, upon learning of their limited means, routed dry cereals and other foods to the Halevys for the remainder of the sail.

One day, towards the end of the fourth week, Faige was resting in the steerage quarters when Kalman came running into the room.

"Mamme, Mamme, come quickly," he shouted. "It's the Statue of Liberty! We can see it. Come quick!"

Faige reached the deck to see Shimon, with Joshua in his arms, staring out at the statue.

"It's even more beautiful than it was the last time I saw it," he said to Faige.

The American flag on the ship had been lowered earlier in the day so it could be raised as the ship was being towed into the harbor. The band struck up *America*, and the crew stood in salute. Shimon and Faige started crying.

"Is this our new home?" Kalman asked.

"Yes," his father answered. "You and Joshua will be real Americans."

NEWARK,
NEW JERSEY

# CHAPTER 20

★

$\mathcal{S}$himon stepped off the dock at Ellis Island and once again saw the Great Hall looming ahead of him. A wave of familiar memories washed over him. For the second time in a decade, he had landed at the shores of America. This time, it was for good.

Shimon guided his family towards the hall and watched Faige gape at the sights around her. He smiled as he recognized his own past fascination reflected in her eyes.

Once in the Great Hall, Shimon was able to use what little English words he remembered to pass quickly through the inspections. Only Joshua's medical exam presented them with a delay.

"What scares me is the number of times the doctors keep examining him," Faige said anxiously. "The first doctor kept him in the room twice as long as he did Kalman. Then he called in a second doctor. Now they have a third doctor in the room. What if they don't allow him into America?"

"Don't be silly," Shimon replied, though he clearly looked as nervous as Faige. "Here's a doctor coming. Maybe he'll tell us something."

The doctor motioned to an interpreter to help him. "Your second son has a heart murmur," he began. "I expect that you are aware of that. Interestingly, he looks and acts quite normal. You'll just have to watch him a little more closely than your other son."

Shimon and Faige were enormously relieved when the doctor dismissed them. They all descended the steps together, dragging their suitcases and clutching their precious admittance papers.

"Tatte, where is Uncle Jacob?" Kalman wondered as he watched his father's eyes wander over the crowd in front of them.

"He should be here any moment," Shimon answered hesitantly. He led his bewildered family in front of the huge building and placed their packages in front of them. They stood there, not knowing what to do.

A carriage driver pulled up and asked Shimon if he wanted a ride to the ferries to Manhattan.

"No, thank you," Shimon answered. "We're waiting for my brother."

"You ought to let me give your family a tour of the island while you're waiting," the driver offered. "I'll take you right by the ferry, and you can see if your brother is there."

"We only have five dollars left," Shimon revealed.

"I'm not doing anything right now," the driver said. "I'll charge you two dollars for a tour of the island for the whole family. I usually charge two dollars per person."

As the driver was speaking, Kalman climbed inside the carriage. "Let's do it, Tatte," he entreated.

"Well, perhaps we'll see Jacob by the ferry," Shimon agreed, and he motioned Faige to board the carriage with Joshua.

The driver then drove the carriage twice around the building, each time in a slightly different way. Within ten minutes, he deposited them back to where they had started. Faige was furious, and Shimon began to argue with the driver when he saw Jacob approaching them. The driver seized the opportunity and drove off as fast as he could.

"I was starting to worry when I didn't see you," Jacob said when he reached them. He gave Shimon a great hug. "I didn't think you would leave without me."

"We thought we would go to the ferry and look for you," Shimon answered.

"You didn't need a carriage for that," Jacob laughed. "The ferry is right in back of the building."

"Well, it looks like we were cheated on our first day in America," Faige said wearily.

As she watched the two brothers embrace, Faige realized how different Jacob looked from the young boy she remembered him as in Skalat. At twenty-six, Jacob was tall and handsome in a way Shimon could never project. He carried with him a self-assurance that was evident in his every gesture. In his fur-trimmed black coat, velvet-lined hat and shiny patent leather shoes, Jacob cut an imposing figure next to his immigrant brother.

Faige looked at her family in dismay. Their clothes were drab even by sober European standards. They looked poor and bedraggled. Faige was wearing the same dress she had worn when she had left Skalat and had slept and travelled in it for more than a month. A not-so-subtle awareness of inferiority crept over her.

"Faige, you're so quiet," Jacob said, shaking Faige out of her reverie.

"I'm just marveling at how different you look," Faige said.

"I would never have recognized you."

"I'm certainly not the same person I was when I left Skalat," Jacob readily admitted.

"Well, you look wonderful, Jacob," Faige gushed. "I'm glad to see you. We wouldn't be here today if it weren't for you."

"There are two things I learned early in life," Jacob responded in ungainly Yiddish. "One is that I have to succeed in America, and the second is that I have to take care of my brother."

Faige stiffened at Jacob's unintentionally condescending remark, while Shimon laughed and heartily hugged his brother again.

Jacob helped carry their meager belongings, and everyone followed him to the dock and onto the ferryboat. The ride to New Jersey was short and pleasant. After they disembarked, Jacob proudly led the way to his new car.

"We should be at your new home soon," Jacob said as they piled in. "It's only around five miles from here. In city driving you're allowed to go thirty miles per hour, but I never go more than twenty."

"That's fast enough for me," Faige exclaimed. She and Kalman were fascinated with their first car ride and strained their necks in every direction to catch all the sights that whizzed by. Only Joshua fell fast asleep.

"Do you remember downtown Newark, Shimon?" Jacob asked.

"How could I forget?" Shimon replied.

"I hope you liked it," Jacob said. "I have rented a three-bedroom apartment for you on Central Avenue and Thirteenth Street."

"Why not something near Prince Street?" Shimon asked.

"Everyone is moving away from Prince Street now," Jacob explained. "Soon there will be nothing left there but the stores.

But you won't have any trouble getting to your *shul* on Barclay and Morton Streets. You can take the Number Twenty-Five bus down Springfield Avenue. On a nice day you can even walk."

Faige was going to ask Jacob where he *davened,* but she quickly caught herself. She surmised that the last time Jacob had been in a *shul* to *daven* had probably been in Skalat.

Jacob stopped the car in front of a large white house directly off Central Avenue on Thirteenth Street.

"What a big house!" Kalman shouted. "Is this where we are going to live?"

"Well, your apartment is on the second floor," Jacob answered. "It has seven rooms and an outside porch. I didn't think you would need three bedrooms, so I thought I would use one of them. Then I can give up the room at the boarding house. The rent there is up to ten dollars a week now. Do you remember, Shimon, it was four when you were here?"

Faige looked at Jacob warily. "How much does this apartment cost?"

"The rent here is thirty dollars a month," said Jacob. "I'll give you ten dollars each month for my room. That should make it easier for you to pay the rent. I've bought some furniture and cooking utensils in order to get you started."

When they entered the apartment, Faige looked around in appreciation. The rooms were large and airy, and the furniture Jacob had bought fit in nicely.

While they started unpacking, Jacob informed them of all the stores nearby.

"Is Mordechai Ehrens still the *shochet* on Prince Street?" Shimon broke in.

"He sure is," Jacob answered. "I saw him the other day and told him you were coming back with your family. He made a loud blessing right in the streets. Both he and Yosef Kagan have moved. I told them where you would be living, and they plan to come see you Saturday afternoon."

Jacob sat down in the easy chair and watched Faige and Shimon unpack.

"Have you decided what you're going to do here, Shimon?" he asked.

"Not yet."

"Well, I'll give Faige some money to get started with until you decide where you are going to work," Jacob said. "There are several grocery stores around here. If you want, I can begin to ask around and see if one of them is for sale. Then I can help you buy it."

Shimon started to thank Jacob but was cut off by Faige. "Jacob, I want to thank you for what you've done for us already," she began, "but I have to be honest with you and my husband. I don't intend ever again to run a business with Shimon. It was bad enough in Skalat where I knew the language and the customs of the people, but even *there* I couldn't stop him from giving merchandise away. How could I run a store with Shimon here?"

Shimon was startled. Faige also looked surprised by her sudden outburst, especially in front of Jacob. During their journey to America, Faige had mulled over this issue for hours. Yet, until she verbalized it now, she hadn't been sure it was the right decision. Something had pushed her in that direction when she met Jacob on Ellis Island. A budding sense of insecurity, however unconscious, had eclipsed her natural sense of assertiveness.

"I've had plenty of time to think this through," Faige went on resolutely. "It has to be this way. Shimon, I'll run our house on the amount of money you bring into it. I'll help you in every way I can, but I'm not going to fight with you as we did in Skalat. We'll have to make our livelihood some other way."

Shimon laughed nervously. "One thing about you," he tossed back a reply, "is that you always let me know, in no uncertain terms, how you feel about something. I guess I have to agree with you. We ought to try something else."

"I think you're both wrong," Jacob interposed. "But it's your life."

Faige was true to her word. She spent the following week setting up the house, while Shimon searched for work. At the end of the week, Shimon came home with some happy news.

"It looks like I found something," he said. "There is a man, Chaim Weiss, whom I had been friendly at *shul* for years when I lived here. He has an acquaintance, Shmuel Gruberman, who has started a charcoal business."

"Starting up a business?" Faige asked apprehensively. "How much will you have to invest?"

"Nothing. That's the good part of this idea. There is almost no money that has to be invested. Mr. Gruberman rents a coal yard on Madison Avenue. Once a week a railroad car pulls into the yard and drops off a carload of charcoal. Mr. Gruberman bags the coal, loads the bags on a wagon and sells them to stores."

"How does this affect you?" Faige asked.

"Gruberman is having trouble selling the coal," Shimon explained. "The coal company will not deliver less than a carload a week, so he needs someone to help him sell it. I would share in the rent for the yard and provide my own horse and wagon. Then we would split the coal deliveries, fill our own bags and sell them. We would each have our own business, but we would share the yard and pay for the coal together."

"That sounds good," Faige answered cautiously. "How much does a horse and wagon cost?"

"Nothing, I hope," Shimon answered. "There are many places around Avon Avenue where you can rent a horse and wagon by the day, week or month. I would rent until I got the money to buy them. There would be almost no investment. Also, I think I would have a natural advantage in selling charcoal bags."

"How is that?"

"Well, Gruberman sells them to hardware and specialty stores. I've spoken to Jacob about it, and he sees no reason why the bags shouldn't be sold in grocery stores. Once they are bagged, the coal isn't too messy, and I have access to grocery stores."

"How?" Faige asked.

"Look at our family," Shimon answered. "The Grosses alone have three large stores in Jersey City, New Brunswick and Elizabeth, and I'm sure they would give the charcoal bags a try. Jacob can possibly help me with some of his accounts, and perhaps even Yosef would. With that nucleus, I have enough to start a business."

While Shimon spent the next few days inquiring about horse rentals, Faige was busy with Kalman. A neighbor had told Faige that Kalman was legally required to go to the public school.

"Isn't there a *cheder* the boy can go to?" Faige asked.

"No, there is none around here," the neighbor answered. "You can hire a rabbi to come to the house and teach him privately, but that is not a substitute for public school. A child of ten has to go to school. That's the law."

Faige did not want to argue with the law. Without even thinking to discuss the matter with Shimon, she set out the next day to Prince Street to buy Kalman school clothes. She bought a pair of knickers, a jacket, shirts, long stockings, a cap and a tie. She also bought a dark flowery dress for herself to replace the frayed garment she had worn out on the journey and splurged on three brightly-colored house dresses at ninety-nine cents each.

The total bill came to fifteen dollars, and Faige noted with dismay that by now she had spent almost half of the fifty dollars Jacob had allotted her. Faige was determined to be more careful with the rest of the money. She did not want to have to go to Jacob for more money before Shimon started to work.

After shopping, Faige took Kalman to the Central Avenue Elementary School to register him for school. The enormous school building contrasted sharply with Faige's vivid recollection of the *cheder* in Skalat. Kalman was likewise awestruck and pulled nervously at his mother's sleeve. Faige smiled at him reassuringly, and the two went in.

Faige had always prided herself on her ability to communicate with different people. She could speak, read and write Yiddish, German, Russian and Polish. But she could not say two words in the language of her new home, a reality she found humiliating.

The principal called in a Yiddish-speaking teacher, Mr. Klein, to serve as interpreter.

"Did Kalman ever attend a secular school?" the principal opened.

"No," Faige answered. "He attended only *cheder*."

"Did he ever study arithmetic?"

"No."

"Does he read any language?"

"Kalman reads Hebrew," Faige said proudly. "He reads his prayers in Hebrew."

"I suppose he never studied science, history or literature," the principal speculated.

"No, he did not," Faige answered, anxiety and embarrassment mounting inside her.

"Well, I have to tell you, Mrs. Halevy, that I see problems with Kalman attending our school."

"Why?" Faige asked plaintively. "Kalman is a fine boy, he is intelligent, kind and well-mannered. Why shouldn't he attend your school?"

"He is too tall," the principal answered simply.

"Too tall?" Faige shouted. "What does that have to do with anything?"

"You needn't get excited, Mrs. Halevy," the principal said. "I'm trying to explain the situation the way I see it. The boy is too tall for the second grade, and yet that is where we should place him according to his learning ability. Chronologically, a boy of ten belongs in the fifth grade, but the work there would be too advanced for him."

Faige was devastated.

"However," the principal concluded, "we cannot legally refuse your son admittance into the school. I recommend he try the fifth grade, and we will see what happens."

Faige and Kalman walked home from the school in silence.

As they reached the block before their home, Kalman finally spoke. "Does this mean I can't go to school, Mamme?"

"No," Faige answered. "It means that school is going to be hard. But we should have expected that. You can't go from Skalat where there are no schools into the schools of America. It's not that easy."

"But why didn't they teach us science and arithmetic in Skalat?" Kalman answered.

"I don't know," Faige replied simply. Faige was beginning to notice that there were many things that weren't taught in Skalat.

As she thought about her old home, a nagging feeling of frustration began to overwhelm her. The obvious contrast between her current position as a poor and ignorant immigrant and her proven standing in Skalat was becoming increasingly disturbing. Faige began doubting whether coming to America had been the right choice. Then she quickly chided herself and remembered that they had just barely arrived.

Faige turned to Kalman. "I think you ought to try this school," she advised. "If it works, fine; if it doesn't, you'll be no worse off than you were before. Just look at your Uncle Jacob. He wasn't much older than you are now when he came to

America. He didn't think of going to school and look how well he is doing."

The following Monday, Kalman attended his first day at school. His teacher, Miss Kurtz, a middle-aged Jewish woman, truly wanted him to succeed and subtly took up his cause. At times she even whispered to him in Yiddish to make it easier for him to follow.

His classmates were not as kind. Only Miss Kurtz's vigilance kept the taunts and laughter in check during class hours. But in the playground after school, Kalman immediately found himself surrounded by a group of jeering students.

"Are sidelocks the latest style in Europe?" one boy asked sarcastically.

"Why don't you go back to the old world and speak Yiddish there?" another boy scorned. "Don't you know English?"

Kalman pushed his *payos* behind his ears and tried to ignore the taunts. Then one conspicuously obnoxious fellow pulled off Kalman's cap, provoking him into a fight. The young Halevy, true to family tradition, pounced on the boy with all his might. In less than a minute, Kalman had easily won. Instantly, the brickbats changed to a guarded respect, which continued during his two years at Central Avenue School.

# CHAPTER 21

★

*E*very *Shabbos* afternoon, Yosef Kagan and Mordechai Ehrens came to visit Shimon and Faige. The *Shabbos* afternoon tradition continued for many years.

The three friends sat around the dining room table, drinking *schnapps* and eating herring and cakes that Faige had baked. While their wives became acquainted, they shared laughs about past adventures and swapped stories of their present endeavors. Shimon cherished these visits. They brought back memories of nostalgic times and deepened the bond of friendship that had spanned a decade and two continents. *Shabbos* was held sacred by the Halevy family and their friends.

For Faige, socializing with seasoned immigrants was a learning experience. The two "Americanized" women willingly shared their expanding knowledge of vital information with Faige. Faige learned which store sold the freshest fish, who had the best prices on knitting yarn and where Mrs. Cohen from down the block got all her expensive clothes on sale. Faige realized that having to cull such information on her own would have taken years of training, a realization that fostered appreciation but also instilled a latent sense of subordination towards the two women.

The week after their second visit, Shimon went into the charcoal business with his partner, Mr. Gruberman, who proceeded to help himself to a good deal more than his rightful share of the earnings. Once again, Shimon was shown to be, in matters of commerce, utterly guileless.

Gruberman's strategy was simple. The coal company delivered a carload of coal to the warehouse on Fridays. The agreement called for Gruberman to make up his bags on Saturday and load them on his wagon, while Shimon would do the same on Sunday. While Shimon observed *Shabbos*, Gruberman doled out more than half of the coal for himself, shortchanging Shimon.

Faige saw through the scam immediately. "Shimon," she said to him, "think about it. How can it be that you sell your share of the coal and make fifteen dollars a week, while your partner sells his share at the same price and makes twenty-five?"

"How do you know he makes that much money?" Shimon asked.

"How do I know?" Faige asked in exasperation. "Everybody knows, everybody except Shimon. We're short money every Friday when the time comes to pay for a new delivery."

Shimon couldn't argue with that. During the week he always had money to give to Faige. It was only on Friday, when he had to pay Gruberman for his share of the next coal shipment, that money was always short.

Rather than tackle the problem of Gruberman, Shimon proposed a solution that shocked Faige and established a pattern of gradual descent into a new Americanization.

"You know," Shimon confided to Faige, "I pay for the horse

and wagon based on a seven-day week, and I never go anywhere on Saturdays."

Faige was aghast. "Don't tell me Shimon Halevy is going to start working on *Shabbos*."

"You know I wouldn't," Shimon said.

"Then what is your plan?" Faige asked.

Shimon hesitated. "Maybe Kalman could work instead," he suggested.

"Kalman?"

"Yes. You see, Kalman approached me with an idea. He wants to work for Abe Friedman on Saturdays using my horse and wagon. Mr. Friedman will load up the wagon with fruits and vegetables, and Kalman would go out and sell them. He might be able to make the ten dollars we are short every week. That way we wouldn't have to ask for more money from Jacob."

Faige was silent. She questioned whether Shimon's antipathy for asking Jacob for more money was the driving factor behind his sanctioning Kalman's working on *Shabbos*. Nonetheless, she was astonished at Shimon's rapid acceptance of the "American way," if not for himself then for his children.

Faige did not know that Shimon had agonized for days over this proposition before presenting it to her. For the previous few Saturdays, though Shimon regularly went to *shul*, and Faige prepared the traditional *Shabbos* meals, the spirit of *Shabbos* that had pervaded their home in Skalat was not duplicated in America. There was no longer that sense of sacredness about the day that they had felt in Skalat, where everyone held the *Shabbos* in awe.

Shimon initially attributed this change to one aspect of the all-encompassing change that had taken over their lives in America. Then he blamed it on the lack of the cohesive Orthodox community that existed in the *shtetls* of Europe. He also blamed it on the fact that Kalman was in a non-Orthodox, even a non-Jewish environment in school, which spilled over into the family's observance of *Shabbos*. Indeed, it had been Kalman's suggestion that he go to work on *Shabbos*. In the end, Shimon no longer blamed it on any particular reason; he no longer felt it necessary to place blame at all. This was just the way it was in America, and he'd have to change and get used to it. The thought crossed his mind that perhaps his commitment to observance in Skalat had also been less than genuine, that perhaps it had been merely a comfortable routine to which he had been accustomed all his life but which really held no deep meaning for him. But the thought was too disturbing, and he blotted it out. He was a good Jew, an observant Jew like his father and his ancestors before him. A little bit of compromise couldn't change that.

Still, Shimon observed Faige's reluctance with anxiety bred of guilt. "It'll only be for a couple of hours during the day," he reasoned. "The rest of the *Shabbos* he wouldn't have to do anything. It's only because we need the money, Faige. If it doesn't work out, he'll stop."

"We'll have to ask Kalman," Faige finally replied with more than a little misgiving. "It will be up to him."

Kalman was not completely shocked by his parents' proposition. He had actually been waiting to see how long it would take for them to realize that America was different from Skalat, and that *Shabbos* meant playing ball with his friends as much as it meant going to *shul*. Still, it was hard for him to understand how his observant parents sanctioned his working on *Shabbos*, while they themselves would not transgress it. He accepted the proposal eagerly, endorsing the notion that it was difficult and unnecessary for a young Jew to follow the old ways in America, family inconsistencies notwithstanding.

The venture was successful. Kalman earned about six dollars every Saturday, which he dutifully turned over to Faige.

She then gave him fifty cents. Kalman's work was in addition to the part-time jobs in groceries he held before and after school. His joint earnings totaled eleven dollars, not an insignificant sum.

With Kalman's earnings, the Halevys managed to cover their monthly expenses. They lived under these circumstances for nearly two years, without having to solicit any help from Jacob.

During those years, Jacob began spending less and less time in the apartment. Besides his traditional breakfast, Shimon and Faige barely saw him, though they did hear the front door squeak on its hinges as it let in Jacob past midnight.

One morning at breakfast, Jacob shocked Shimon and Faige with an unexpected announcement. "I'm going to get married next spring, before *Pesach*," he revealed.

Faige and Shimon were stunned. After an elongated silence, Shimon finally responded. "You're getting married? I didn't know you were seeing anyone. This was the best kept secret in all of Newark. *Mazel tov!* Do we know the bride?"

"No, I'm sure you don't know her," Jacob continued. "Her name is Shirley Gellis. She's an only child, and her parents have lived in Newark for many years. They are not immigrants. Shirley was born here, and her father was born here. That makes Shirley a third-generation American."

Faige lifted her eyebrows in mock admiration and made a caustic remark about Jacob's formidable social advance. "Is that why we haven't met her?" she then asked.

Jacob pushed back his chair indignantly.

Shimon cast a castigating look at his wife and turned to Jacob. "How long have you known her?" he asked, trying to change the subject. "You never mentioned her before. We haven't even met her yet."

"Well, I couldn't exactly bring Shirley here," Jacob answered flatly.

"Oh, of course not," Faige agreed, shaking her head in obvious exaggeration.

Jacob looked at Faige. "I didn't say anything was wrong with you," he defended himself, realizing he had gone a little too far. "You're just different, and that's not your fault."

"I guess we'll meet her at the wedding," Shimon remarked.

"Oh, I suppose you'll see her long before that," Jacob answered nonchalantly. "I'm just not sure how I'll go about doing it. I'm telling you about my marriage now, because it is going to affect you."

Faige looked at him suspiciously. "How is that?"

"I'll be moving out around a month from now, sometime in January."

"I don't understand," Shimon said. "Didn't you say you were getting married before *Pesach*? Why should you move out so soon? Where will you stay?"

"I bought a large property on Avon Avenue and Thirteenth Street, only about a mile away from here," Jacob answered, trying hard not to look smug. "It has a big, two-family house and thirteen garages."

"Thirteen garages!" Shimon exclaimed. "Why do you need so many garages?"

"I'm organizing the Capitol Butter and Egg Company on that piece of property," Jacob announced proudly. "Shirley and I will live in the house. The garages will be the warehouse. We're also going to convert two of the garages into a walk-in refrigerator. That's the way of the future. No more ice. It's too messy."

Jacob sat back in his chair and looked at his brother and sister-in-law. The three sat in an awkward silence.

"Well, *mazel tov*, Jacob," Faige finally said. "I hope everything works out for you."

After Jacob left, Shimon and Faige sat for a long time without saying anything.

Faige didn't even look at her husband. "I told you Jacob was ashamed of us," she said at last. "But I never knew how much so until now. It seems his biggest problem, with all his plans, is how to introduce his fiancee to us. Do you know what this means, Shimon?"

"No."

"If there is soon to be a wedding, there had to have been an engagement," Faige pointed out logically. "We weren't invited to whatever they had, and in fact, we didn't even know about it. Can you imagine that, Shimon? Your own brother lives in one house with you, and you didn't even know when he became engaged."

"Take it easy," Shimon responded. "It's not such a big deal compared to all the other good things Jacob has done for us."

However, Shimon didn't sound or look too convincing. It wasn't the first argument over Jacob's pretensions that Shimon and Faige had. But for the first time, though he wouldn't admit it, Shimon was beginning to see that Faige might be right in her assessment of his brother.

Jacob moved out of the apartment and into his new home in January, but he continued to go to his brother's house for breakfast every working day.

Since Jacob would no longer be renting his room, Shimon and Faige began to consider a move to a cheaper apartment. Shimon found one at 142 Peshine Avenue and arranged to move the following month.

Peshine Avenue was densely populated and was almost equally divided among Italians, Poles and Jews. Set over a candy store, the apartment cost only nineteen dollars a month.

Shimon loved Peshine Avenue, while Faige was initially confused by it. Kalman and Joshua were easily swept up by the street's exciting lifestyles.

A week after they had moved in, Jacob approached Faige with an olive branch in hand. "Would it be all right if I bring Shirley over next *Shabbos* for lunch?" he inquired.

"Of course," came the magnanimous reply. "We would be very happy to meet her."

Faige spent the rest of the week scouring the apartment, washing the floors and mopping the kitchen linoleum. Every piece of furniture was cleaned and waxed three times.

"I am sure Shirley is not going to look there," Shimon laughed. "Only Cossacks would bother, and their concern wasn't cleanliness."

"Most likely she won't check," answered Faige, "but I want everything perfect. Tomorrow, I'm going to do the windows."

"That's ridiculous, Faige," Shimon remonstrated.

"I don't want to give your brother's fiancee any reason to be ashamed of us," Faige rationalized.

The work paid off. Shirley, a charming and gracious young lady, was impressed. "Your apartment is lovely, Faige," she said. "And your cooking is superb. I don't know why Jacob thought I might not like it."

"He was afraid some of our 'green' would show," Faige answered with some residual sarcasm.

Shirley smiled, not noting resentment in Faige's remark. "I see your English is not so bad," she commented.

Faige laughed. "It's not so good either. I never speak English in the house, although Kalman answers me in English when I talk to him in Yiddish."

"Kalman," Shirley repeated the name, as if hearing it for the first time. "There should be an American version of that. How about Kenneth or Ken for short? That sounds right, Jacob, doesn't it?"

Jacob nodded. Surprisingly, Faige smiled, too, not feeling insulted at this intrusion.

Shirley was encouraged. "Shimon would sound better as Sam," she continued, "and Faige could be Fannie. I don't think we have to change Joshua. That name sounds dignified."

Despite her feelings towards Jacob, Faige was truly pleased with Jacob's choice, and she and Shimon looked forward to the wedding in April.

When the day arrived, Jacob brought Shimon and his family to the Conservative synagogue in his car.

"I am very thankful you're both here," Jacob confided. "It would be awful for me to marry without you. You're the only family I have here."

"If it weren't for you, Jacob, we wouldn't even be here," Shimon replied.

"So we both have something to be thankful for," Faige concluded. *"Mazel tov!"*

# CHAPTER 22

★

As America roared through the Twenties, oblivious to the market crash that would soon write a wretched epitaph to the decade, the nation enjoyed the good times while they lasted.

Shimon and Faige Halevy did not share in the evanescent prosperity. Shimon continued to work long, hard hours making little profit in return.

Faige was now expecting a new child and was tempted to reconsider her decision not to go into business with Shimon. Though she had tackled many of the hurdles in acclimating herself to her new world, making progress with the language, too, Faige wanted to avoid confrontations with her husband over work matter and determined not to overrule her instincts on the matter.

After Jacob's wedding and then *Pesach*, she devoted her energies to making the home function on a small budget and preparing for Kalman's upcoming *bar-mitzvah* in September.

"I think we'll have to settle for a *kiddush* at the *shul*," Faige told Shirley one day when they were discussing plans. "I would like to have a party in the house after *davening*, but it would be too difficult and expensive."

"You do whatever you want, and we'll help you," Shirley answered. "I think under the circumstances a *kiddush* is fine."

Faige was flustered. She hadn't confessed the hardship of the expense to solicit help from her sister-in-law. It was difficult for her to ask anyone for help or even intimate such a request. Nevertheless, she was grateful.

"Thank you, Shirley, but we'll really try to make the most of what we can afford. We can make the *kiddush* practically a sit-down lunch," Faige said, hoping to recast the modest affair into something more sizable. "Shimon has known the men at *shul* for a long time, and it's our first *simchah* in America. It's our opportunity to pay back some of the kindnesses to people who have helped us."

"I think it's remarkable how you and Sam are concerned with your social position in the synagogue while at the same time you're working with a small income," Shirley said, rather ingenuously. "There is no shame in not being able to afford a large *bar-mitzvah*. I don't know why you feel you have to invite the entire congregation to the *kiddush*."

Faige was indignant. The intimation of their using the *kiddush* as a means of aggrandizing their status was disparaging. Besides, she wondered, how do you invite only part of a congregation to a *kiddush*?

Faige later told Shimon about her conversation with Shirley.

"That shows how much she knows about *shuls*," Shimon laughed. "I have been in *shuls* all my life, and I've never seen or heard of a *kiddush* made for only part of the congregation."

A week before the *bar-mitzvah*, Shimon finally asked Kalman what he had learned.

"Not much," Kalman responded.

"What do you mean, not much?" Shimon answered angrily. "You've been learning with the rabbi for almost a year now."

"First of all, he is not a rabbi," Kalman retorted, "although he makes me call him that. Rabbi Hest is the *shammash* in your *shul*."

"Well, you could still learn from him," Shimon countered.

"Not really. Rabbi Hest falls asleep every time I read my *haftorah*. He's never heard a word of it. Sometimes I stop in the middle and just sit there for the longest time, and Rabbi Hest doesn't even know the difference."

Shimon saw his investment had yielded little return. "Are you telling me, a week before your *bar-mitzvah*, you will not be able to say the *haftorah*?"

"No, I'm not saying that at all," Kalman replied. "I can say the *haftorah*. I knew how much it meant to you and Mamme, so I taught it to myself. I know it as well as any of the other *bar-mitzvah* boys, even better than some of them."

Shimon could not conceal his smile. "So you know your *haftorah*, and you taught it to yourself," he mused. "You should have told us. All this while we have been giving money to Rabbi Hest for nothing."

The following week, Kalman was as good as his word. He performed his *haftorah* beautifully. Faige sat in the women's balcony, swelling with love and pride. Here was her eldest son with whom she had been through hardship, war, loneliness and even death. Faige thought of the world she had left behind in Skalat, and tears trickled down her cheeks at the realization that the people who had meant the most to her could not share in her happiness now.

Shimon was too busy entertaining congratulations from his friends to lament the lack of family. He discreetly told Mordechai and Yosef that Kalman had taught himself the *haftorah*.

"That's amazing!" Mordechai said. "With a head like that he should go to a *yeshivah*. There is no telling what he can become."

Kalman was never given that opportunity; to send him to *yeshivah* would involve great sacrifice, and he was needed at home. And public school seemed not to provide any incentive for him either. He was not progressing in his studies, and he lacked the motivation to keep with it. It wasn't long after his *bar-mitzvah* that Kalman contemplated leaving school.

"I don't see how we can stop him," Shimon told Faige. "There is no point in his going to school. It's really not his fault. There was too much for him to catch up with. He started too late."

"I think Abe Friedman has something to do with Kalman's sudden desire to leave school," Faige said, referring to a grocer who had made Kalman a job offer with some rather unusual hours. "Working from four in the afternoon to midnight hardly seems like normal grocery store hours to me."

"You're right," Shimon agreed. "Where is Kalman now?"

"He's on the street playing with some friends," Faige said. "I told him he can stay out until ten. He'll be up soon, and we'll talk to him."

Kalman didn't return until almost eleven that night, after both his parents had gone to bed.

His mother confronted him the following morning. "Where were you last night?" she demanded.

"What do you mean?" Kalman responded with some surprise. "You know where I was, down on the street." His mother rarely sought an accounting of his free time.

Faige looked closely at her son. "Tatte and I wanted to talk to you, but you didn't come upstairs until after ten o'clock."

"It was only a little after," Kalman quibbled.

"It was closer to eleven," Faige said impatiently. "I heard you come in, but I didn't want to disturb your father."

Kalman said nothing.

Faige pointed to the cellar door. "I want you to come down to the cellar with me."

"Why is that?" Kalman looked surprised.

"I'll tell you when we get there," Faige assured him.

Kalman ran after his mother, who was already halfway down the steps. When they both reached the bottom, Faige pointed a finger at a neatly packaged carton that had been deliberately placed in a remote corner of the cellar.

"What is that?" Faige asked accusingly.

"Oh, that," Kalman said, looking slightly bewildered. "One of my friends asked me to keep it for a little while."

"What's in the box?"

"I don't know!"

"What do you mean, you don't know?" Faige demanded. "You take a box like that from somebody and hide it in our cellar without even knowing what it is? It might be something stolen."

Kalman looked shocked. "I never thought of that, Mom," he stammered.

"Well, you *have* to think of it," Faige retorted. "I want you to return the box immediately. Now, come upstairs. I want to talk to you."

Back in the kitchen, Faige sat down at the table. "I want to know three things, Kalman," she began. "First, what is this business about your leaving school? Second, what exactly is the job offer Abe Friedman gave to you? And third, why didn't you talk to me about it?"

"I didn't talk to you because I haven't decided anything yet," Kalman said honestly, still standing. "Besides, the offer from Mr. Friedman just came the other day. Papa was there, and he heard it. He must have told you about it."

"Yes, Tatte told me about the job," Faige acknowledged, "but he doesn't understand it any more than I do. What kind of work can it be in a grocery store from four to midnight? Those aren't normal store hours."

"Well, it isn't a normal store job," Kalman admitted. "That's why I'm still thinking about it."

"If it isn't a normal job, then what kind of a job is it?" Faige demanded, her eyes narrowing suspiciously.

"It's a sort of delivery job," Kalman answered lamely.

"A delivery job in a grocery store that's done at night?" Faige asked.

Kalman sat down at the table opposite his mother. "We have to deliver at night," he said. "That's why the job starts at sunset. We deliver to bootleggers."

"Bootleggers!" Faige cried. "Who on earth are they?"

"They are the people who make liquor for resale," Kalman explained a bit smugly, aware of his superiority to his mother in such matters of world knowledge. "America has a Prohibition law. That means that you can't buy liquor. But you can't tell that from the streets around Prince Street. There are dozens of places where they make liquor. It's an open secret. But none of these distilleries want to attract too much attention. That's why all the deliveries have to be made at night."

Faige looked astonished and pondered this information for a silent minute. "Mr. Friedman does this?" she finally asked. "He sells ingredients to bootleggers to make liquor? I can't believe it, he seems like such a nice man."

"He *is* a nice man," Kalman confirmed. "That's why I'd like to work for him. Mr. Friedman will pay me four dollars a night, Monday through Friday. That's twenty dollars a week."

"What does Mr. Friedman sell to the bootleggers?" asked Faige.

"Mostly sugar, corn and syrup. The boxes aren't really too big, but sometimes you have to carry them up a long flight of stairs." Kalman looked squarely at his mother. "Look, Mom,

I'm almost thirteen-and-a-half. School is a waste of time. I have to start doing something."

Faige didn't know what to say. She was pleased that Kalman was eager to work, but she still didn't quite understand what Prohibition was, let alone bootleggers.

"I'll talk to Tatte," she finally said. "We'll tell you what to do."

Shimon and Faige's need for money, especially with the impending birth of a baby in the family, and their basic ignorance of the law led to their consent to Kalman's job with Mr. Friedman. Kalman was happy with the work, and his parents were happy with the money.

In January of that year, Faige gave birth to a baby girl in the bedroom of their new apartment on Peshine Avenue. They named her Leah.

When Leah was born, Joshua found himself supplanted as the baby of the family. Not particularly mindful of status, Joshua welcomed Leah rather indifferently, already immersed in activities outside the home.

Unlike Kalman, who by nature and circumstance was more serious, Joshua was a cheerful, carefree boy who had never known what it was like not to be an American.

Joshua attended the Morton Street Synagogue, which was a fairly inexpensive school that had a dual curriculum of Jewish and English studies. His parents were happy to send at least one of their sons to a Jewish school, and Joshua seemed to enjoy the Jewish studies. Schoolwork came easily to him. Still, Joshua's grades did not reflect his aptitude. He established a scholastic routine that would last throughout high school, giving his studies just enough thought to get by.

Several months into the school year, Shimon had boasted to his friends at the *shul* about his son's scholastic achievements. One *Shabbos* morning before *davening*, Shimon opened a *siddur*, and Joshua was summoned to read aloud before several men. He read poorly and tentatively, and the chagrined Shimon did not even try to help him through the ordeal.

Shimon closed the *siddur*. "So, you don't know how to read after all," he said in utter disappointment.

Joshua was crestfallen. He practiced his reading every day after that until he became the best reader in his class. But it was too late. Shimon never again called him for a public reading.

Joshua did not give up on performing, however. Presumably because he was tall and heavy-set, he was given all the lead parts in the class plays. He was King Achashverosh in the *Purim* play and one of the Hasmoneans in the *Chanukah* show. For these occasions, Faige bought remnants of material, from which she sewed Joshua's costumes, at times staying up until the early hours of the morning to finish them.

After school hours, Joshua spent his time playing outside his house with a group of twenty to forty boys on Peshine Avenue. They played football, softball, baseball and marbles. They made wooden guns and formed go-carts from wooden boxes with axles and wheels taken from carriages. Joshua was busy until nightfall, when he would return home with scrapes and bruises and holes in his pockets.

# CHAPTER 23

★

That summer, Shirley told Shimon and Faige that she was expecting a child. After offering congratulations and best wishes, Faige told her that she was also expecting.

In November, Shirley gave birth to a baby boy and named him Robert. A little more than two months later, Faige gave birth to a boy, Moshe.

Despite the hectic schedule in the Halevy household, one thing remained constant—the problem of money. Shimon's charcoal business was deteriorating, and Faige was receiving less and less money to manage the house. Had it not been for Kalman's earnings, the Halevy family would not have been able to survive without asking for outside help.

Now sixteen, Kalman continued to work four nights a week for Abe Friedman. He was up to five dollars per night and very proud of his pay. His mother told him he was making almost as much as his father, but Kalman believed he was actually making more, because Shimon never knew what his net profit was.

Shimon's financial situation was exacerbated one afternoon in December, after a particularly harsh snow storm. As Shimon tried to scale the hill on Hawthorne Avenue from Bergen Street to Osborne Terrace, the horse he had rented for his charcoal deliveries slipped on the ice and fell to the pavement. The police came, shot the injured horse and cited Shimon with a violation. He was accused of cruelty to animals.

The stable owner sought to recoup the value of his horse, and Shimon agreed to an out-of-court settlement that did not define his liability. Besides being deeply ashamed of the citation, Shimon was still paying five dollars a week for the dead horse for the full following year.

Faige found her own way of solving Shimon's obligation to the stable owner. She accepted a bachelor as her boarder for the price of five dollars per week. The fee included board and some meals. But the boarding solution did not last as long as Faige had anticipated.

"Tell me, Mr. Goldberg," Faige asked, as she served him breakfast one morning. "What time did you go to bed last night?"

Visibly taken aback by the question, the man struggled for an answer.

"It must have been after eleven," Faige continued, without waiting for a reply. "I heard you drawing the water for your bath at ten o'clock."

"That sounds about right," Mr. Goldberg agreed.

Faige was furious. "How can you start a bath at ten o'clock at night during the week in our house? That's when we all go to bed. The running water keeps us up. You're living in a house with children. And then you walk around from room to room as if it's the middle of the day. My husband works hard and needs his rest."

"But, Faige," the man interrupted, "even if I agreed with you that it was too late to take a bath at ten, I couldn't get the bathroom any earlier. Certainly I couldn't have any privacy."

"If you want privacy, Mr. Goldberg, you'll have to go somewhere else," Faige declared. "If you stay here, you have to do things when we do them. I know that it isn't easy. We're a busy house, but you haven't suffered by being with us. You can take a bath now, and no one would stop you."

"Yes, but now I have to go to work," Mr. Goldberg answered with an abridged smile.

The two concluded their conversation on friendly terms, but both knew the problem was not resolved. Faige knew she could not force Goldberg to leave. It would be easier to move to a new location that simply would not include him.

Faige's choice was the first floor apartment of a two-family house almost at the corner of Peshine, a few houses off Clinton Avenue. She extolled the apartment to Shimon.

"You'll love it," she raved. "After living in four-family houses, it will be as if we have our own home. The yard is large and fenced in. I can put Leah and Moshe out there for fresh air. We'll have the same number of rooms, but I think they are larger. Best of all, we get a free paint job when we move in."

"It sounds all right to me," Shimon answered. "I wonder how the kids will like it, although it shouldn't make any difference to them. It's still the same street."

There was another unanticipated dividend to the move. Unlike Prince Street, Clinton Avenue had dignity. The houses were principally fashioned in brick, were well-maintained and housed many communal institutions. The street was clean and active and reminded Faige of the much wider streets of downtown Newark.

Faige enjoyed strolling on Clinton Avenue with Moshe and Leah, gazing at the elegant homes and tilting her chin upwards when passing someone on the street, as if to say, "I live here, too." Whenever anyone asked Kalman or Joshua where they lived, they would always reply "off Clinton Avenue" and then wait for the ever so subtle lift of the eyebrows they inevitably received.

Despite their strains at appearances, however, the Halevys' financial situation was declining. Shimon's coal business was contracting steadily even before Black Thursday, that infamous day in October of 1929 when billions of dollars were lost overnight and thousands of accounts wiped out.

As coal companies intensified their attempts to power sales, they sought to eliminate local competition and staged a price war Shimon could not win. Bags of charcoal that were selling for five cents a bag cost Shimon eight cents even before factoring his labor and overall expenses.

Mr. Gruberman recognized the dilemma immediately. "We waited too long," he told Shimon. "We should have sold out to the companies while we had something to sell. Now we are stuck, and the only thing we can do is close our business."

"Don't be too hasty," Shimon cautioned. "The whole situation could change overnight. The coal companies are too big to want to sell directly to the stores. They don't have the personnel and the structure for the operation. I'm going to hold on and wait for something good to happen."

It wasn't long until Shimon was finally forced out of business. Mr. Gruberman offered the coal company his route if they would hire him to manage it, and the company gladly acquiesced. Shimon found himself alone in the yard, forced to sell the entire delivery of coal at a time when he was charging three cents a bag higher than the retail price.

Jacob heard of his brother's plight and offered to help. "Close the yard, give up your horse and wagon, and come to work for me."

"What will I do there?" Shimon asked.

"You'll work in the warehouse," Jacob answered quickly. "I

have two men there now, but I need a third."

Shimon did not look excited at the proposition.

Jacob tried to assuage his reluctance. "There is no other job you can do," he said rather callously. "You're not a salesman. You can't drive a car or a truck, so you couldn't be a driver. The other position we have is an egg candler. He looks inside the egg in a darkroom to check for blood spots or double yolks. It's a specialized job, and it's not for you."

"All right," Shimon agreed dispassionately. "I'll work in the warehouse."

"I'll pay you eighteen dollars a week," Jacob said, looking more at the floor than at his brother. "Will that be all right?"

"If that's what you pay, it will have to be all right," Shimon reluctantly responded.

"We work from eight in the morning to around six at night," Jacob informed his brother. "I only work the men later if it's absolutely necessary. We also work until two or three on Saturdays. For now, I will make an exception for you. Later, I'll expect you to stay some evenings to make up for it."

Faige and Kalman were astounded at the conditions Shimon had committed himself to.

"I think the job is ridiculous!" Faige concluded resentfully. "You're going to make a slave of yourself with all those hours for less money than Kalman makes right now."

"Kalman's is a specialized job," Shimon answered tersely but without conviction.

"Pop, my job isn't that specialized. It's nothing you couldn't do," Kalman pointed out. "Besides, don't you see Uncle Jacob never promised you anything better than the warehouse job? If you stay with him all of your life, you'll be in the same job doing the same work."

"And probably for the same money," added Faige.

"Stop that talk, both of you," Shimon answered angrily. "I

don't feel either of you is grateful enough for everything Jacob has done for us."

Shimon stalked out of the room, leaving Faige and Kalman staring at each other despondently. They knew Shimon did not want the job any more than they did, but his stubborn regard for his brother closed the door of opportunity in his face and theirs. They spent the next few weeks trying to persuade him to look elsewhere but met with no success.

Thus Shimon went to work for his brother. He made arrangements to give up his horse and wagon by the end of 1929 and began working for Jacob after the first of that new year.

It did not take long for Shimon to get used to his new job. He rather enjoyed the work and especially liked his white long coat, an expression of cleanliness that was nicely juxtaposed to his sooty labors with coal.

His job was devoted to readying eggs for inspection and sale. He unloaded them, thirty dozen to a case, from the trucks that brought the eggs from the suppliers. Shimon separated the cases according to size and then positioned them for the egg candlers. The candlers examined the inside of the eggs by a light in an otherwise darkened room. After the eggs were candled, Shimon boxed them, one dozen to a carton, and repacked them. He was also expected to help unload and load trucks with any and all merchandise.

Shimon's strength was more than adequate to his responsibilities. He easily was able to "toss around" the egg cases, and the work's pure physicality freed him from his erstwhile worries of prices and customers. But Shimon missed the outdoor life that work with coal required, and he missed his horse and wagon. And after a few weeks, the monotony of the job and the confining space of his worksite became oppressing.

The senior egg candler, Mr. Cooper, soon took Shimon into his confidence. "Tell your brother you want to become an egg candler," he advised. "It's the best job in the place. The work is not as hard, and we're the only union employees in the company. I make thirty-five a week. I'll bet that's almost twice what the warehouse people make."

"My brother has me doing what he wants me to do," Shimon confessed with false congeniality.

But after a few weeks, Shimon began to side with Mr. Cooper. He told Jacob that he wanted to become an egg candler.

"Forget it," Jacob said. "That is a highly skilled job. You could never do it."

Wanting to avoid a confrontation, Shimon did not contest Jacob's condescending rebuff. Even Faige's fervent entreaties couldn't induce Shimon to challenge his brother's decision. Shimon held his tongue, and the years dragged by as he continued to work for Jacob on Jacob's terms.

# CHAPTER 24

★

$\mathcal{B}$y the spring of 1930, Kalman was eighteen, and he realized it was time to change jobs. There was now little reason for the nightly deliveries to the bootleggers. Their commerce was taken for granted, and the need for clandestine shipments waned. Kalman had held onto this night job in addition to the hours he put in during the day, doing odd jobs in various grocery stores.

School had been abandoned long ago, though Kalman had little regrets about not furthering his education. He knew Skalat had put him behind in learning, but the disadvantage would not have been an insurmountable one had he really wanted to succeed in school. He was never pushed in that direction by his parents, mainly because they needed his income, and he never thought to pursue something that would have conflicted with his family's needs.

Kalman hardly ever complained. He never protested against working and never asked for more of the rightful share of his earnings than his parents gave him. It was an understood rule that his job was to help support the family, and he did his job well.

But sometimes, when Faige would hear Kalman come home late at night from his delivery job, she would wake with a mingling feeling of appreciation and guilt. Shaking her head at the clock, she would get out of bed to give Kalman something to eat and drink before he went to sleep. While Kalman regaled his mother with stories about Abe Friedman's store, an inaudible sigh would invariably escape his mother, and Kalman knew that it was meant for him.

Kalman's parents wanted their son to succeed, and looking at his prospects now, they realized a decision would have to be made about his future. It was time for Kalman to visit Uncle Jacob.

When Kalman detailed his situation to his uncle, Jacob sat back in his office chair and looked at his nephew. Kalman was growing up beautifully. He had the handsome Halevy appearance and was tall and strong like his father. He also shared Shimon's mild disposition. Jacob could not recall a single instance where Kenneth, as he liked to think of him, was not polite and respectful.

"I agree you should leave Abe," Jacob said. "There is no future for you there. Now that you're eighteen, you ought to start seriously learning the grocery business. The store where you're working now has too limited an operation."

Kalman nodded his head in assent and waited for his uncle to suggest something.

"I think the best you can do for yourself, Ken," Jacob continued, "is to learn the food business as thoroughly as possible, from the ground up. You should do what I did when I first came to this country. I worked for your cousin, Martin Gross in Jersey City. He has a fairly large store, and it's a good place to learn the business. If you would like, I will talk to him about you and see what he says."

Kalman was not at all enthused at the prospect of working for Martin Gross. He recalled his father's stories about the man and his blind devotion to his store. Martin was willing to work twenty hours a day to generate a successful business. He also expected a similar fervor from his employees.

Still, Kalman did not have any other opportunities available, especially in the hard economic times gripping the country at the time.

"Thank you, Uncle," he told Jacob. "I know you have my best interests in mind."

Kalman began to work for Martin Gross in April, right after *Pesach*, and was to stay until December of 1936. Jacob's prediction that Kalman would learn the grocery business was fulfilled at a fierce cost. Kalman's week was divided into two parts. From Monday through Wednesday, he worked from seven in the morning to eight at night, and from Thursday through Saturday, from seven in the morning to two in the afternoon, a total of sixty hours per week.

The store was a compressed version of the larger food stores that were evolving at the time. It had separate dairy and meat counters, a corner assigned for fruits and vegetables, and the others stocked with grocery items, haphazardly stacked on shelves and floors. Kalman chiefly supervised the dairy counter, remained unchanged throughout his entire stay there.

Kalman was a diligent and hard worker. Yet he marvelled at his co-workers' dedication. After all, he was a cousin and was expected to have the welfare of the store foremost in his mind. But there were two Polish employees who worked just as hard and voiced few complaints as well. This was proof to Kalman that the Depression was truly severe.

The second floor on top of the store housed the family's

living quarters. Its kitchen was unusually large and always busy. Food was everywhere and meant to be easily obtainable. In this oddly communal arrangement, both the family and the workers were supposed to eat meals, but the workers typically ate sandwiches while working.

After work at night, Kalman did not bother going home to Newark. He slept his few hours each night in makeshift accommodations given to him in Jersey City. Several cots were strewn about the three bedrooms on the second level of the store. They were the ad hoc beds of the workers who chose to sleep over on the store's busiest nights. For Kalman, those nights were every night.

On Sunday, Kalman usually returned home around noon and spent the rest of the day resting for the resumption of his ordeal on Monday morning. He brought home his wages of twenty dollars each week, from which he would receive five dollars. That stupendous sum, however, had to finance his bus fare to Jersey City for the week and some meals as well. Though they said nothing, Shimon and Faige commiserated with their son's ordeal. In particular, they were bothered by Kalman's working on *Shabbos*, but they saw this as part of their sacrifice. But they could not subsist on Shimon's meager eighteen dollars a week, so what could they do?

While he did not complain, one thing seemed clear to Kalman, as it did to the rest of the Halevy children. Kalman received almost none of the classic childhood perquisites, such as toys, bicycles and sporting equipment, that other children did. Joshua received slightly more than Kalman, and Leah and Moshe received a bit more than he. Thus, Joshua received a skateboard that Kalman was to envy into his adult life, and Leah received a bicycle that almost devastated Joshua.

While Kalman labored for his cousin, nine-year-old Joshua got by in school, doing little work outside the classroom. Joshua was now attending the Avon Avenue School. The school at the Morton Street Synagogue that Joshua had attended became a casualty of economic conditions, and Joshua had been transferred.

Young as he was, however, Joshua missed the Jewish curriculum. He missed the stories about the *parshah* of the week, the plays they had put on about the upcoming holidays and the songs he had learned in Hebrew. He asked his parents to be sent to another Jewish school.

"The only other school I can think of is the afternoon school at Morton Street," Shimon said to Faige.

"I'm not sending him to Morton Street for afternoon school," Faige responded. "It's too far, and besides it's unnecessary."

"Then where can he go?" Shimon asked.

"He'll go to Temple Bnai Abraham," Faige said matter-of-factly. "They have a beautiful school building, and the principal is Abraham Ehrens, Mordechai's brother. The only thing wrong with it is that they charge two dollars a week, and that's too much."

"Of course it's too much," Shimon agreed, contesting the tuition sum but not the prospect of his son attending a Conservative day school. The Halevy family commitment to the Judaism of their ancestors was unravelling even further. What was forbidden to Shimon had been allowed for Kalman—and now for Joshua as well. "I'll talk to Abraham. I know him slightly. Maybe he'll take less if he knows we can't afford the regular tuition."

Abraham Ehrens took in Joshua at a dollar twenty-five a week. Shimon and Faige were pleased with their bargain, and Joshua was happy to learn Hebrew again, even though they taught him things he had learned a little differently two years earlier at Morton Street.

The single curriculum at the Avon Avenue School seemed

simple to Joshua, who was experienced at juggling more than twice the formal public school demands. But Joshua continued to spend time playing ball after school instead of doing homework, thus never receiving higher than average grades.

Faige had to answer for her son's mediocrity at the first PTA meeting she attended at the new school. Unlike her experiences at similar meetings in the day school, where she could always fall back on her Yiddish, Faige found herself struggling to express her thoughts in English.

"You ask me why Joshua doesn't do homework," Faige began uncertainly. "I don't know. He never brings any books home, never. 'Where are your books?' I ask him. 'In school,' he tells me."

"Do you ever see him do his homework?" the teacher asked.

"I ask. I ask," Faige replied, shaking her head vigorously. "He tells me he did it already. I ask him when he did it. He says, 'In the lunchroom when I was eating.' I tell him, 'This is no good. In the lunchroom, you are supposed to eat lunch. At home you do homework.'"

"Calm yourself," the teacher interjected. "Many students do their homework during their lunch period. It's not unusual. It's just that Joshua only does work in the lunchroom. Even compositions that were assigned over a long period of time are handed in as if they were done the same day at lunch. I just feel it's a shame, because he could do so much better."

Faige was indignant when she came home that night, and Joshua promised to try harder. He really did, for about two weeks. Then he relapsed into his previous conduct and made good use of the lunchroom again.

Joshua almost paid dearly for his remiss behavior. In the spring, Joshua's class was chosen to perform a play in the auditorium in front of the entire school. Its theme was cleanliness, and Joshua was selected to be King Soap.

The day before the scheduled performance, Faige told Joshua that she intended to keep him out of school the next day to buy him new clothes for *Pesach*.

"Mom, I have a big part in the play tomorrow," Joshua told his mother. "I can't be absent."

"What do you mean you can't be absent?" his mother retorted. "This is the first I'm hearing about a play. If it had been so important, I would have heard about it before."

"Mom, please listen to me," Joshua pleaded. "It's in the auditorium for the whole school to see. I can't be absent."

"At Morton Street they always informed me when you were in a play," Faige pointed out. "You're exaggerating, as you always do. Tomorrow is the best day I have to go shopping with you, and so we are going."

There was nothing Joshua could do to change her mind. The play was scheduled for two the next afternoon. At twelve-thirty, Joshua and Faige were on Prince Street, carrying a bag with Joshua's new suit, two white shirts, a tie and a navy blue cap. Joshua looked at the clock on a nearby store and renewed his call to his mother to take him to school.

"Go to school now? That's ridiculous!" she said. "We wouldn't get there until almost two o'clock."

"There is just a chance we can still make it," Joshua insisted.

"How would we go?" Faige asked hesitatingly.

"We're right by Springfield Avenue. We can take the Number Twenty-Six bus to Seymour Avenue and walk over to Avon. We might just make it."

The vacillating Faige allowed herself to be pushed onto the bus. They arrived at the school at one-thirty, whereupon Joshua immediately tugged his mother backstage of the auditorium.

When his classmates and teachers saw Joshua, they began to applaud. "He's here, he's here!" they shouted.

Faige was shown to a seat in the audience, and Joshua took

his place on the throne set up for King Soap. Joshua performed well, and his mother was not sorry she had been dragged along.

Several weeks later, on the first anniversary of the move to their new home on Peshine Avenue, the landlord announced a rent increase.

Faige was shocked. "But Mr. Klein, we've only lived here a year. Why are you raising our rent?"

"I have to, Faige," Mr. Klein replied abruptly. "My taxes went up a lot, and you have to share the raise with me. It isn't as if you are living in a four-family house any more. Individually, their taxes went up less than mine. I have no choice. I'll have to raise your rent to twenty-eight dollars a month."

"But we're only paying twenty-two now," Faige pointed out. "That's a six-dollar increase."

"You ought to realize that you're enjoying luxury living, and you have to pay for it," Mr. Klein contended. "A two-family house is not a four-family house. The back yard alone is worth the difference. If you don't like it, you can move. I'll have no problem renting the apartment for at least twenty-eight or thirty a month. Maybe I'll even get thirty-five."

Faige was devastated at first, but she soon righted her flagging composure. "We'll just have to move again," she confided to Shimon. "But I think it's time to leave Peshine Avenue. I don't want to go back to the four-family houses. Maybe we can find the same kind of a house on a less popular street."

"I don't have to be near the stables any more, so that should help," Shimon pointed out. "Jacob or somebody else could take me to work from wherever we live. Start looking. You'll come up with something."

It took Faige less than a week to find the family's next home. It was at 11 Marie Place. Faige was delighted it was another two-family house. It was a spacious apartment with two large bedrooms and a sun parlor that could be used as a third bedroom.

"Can you imagine," Faige began, "for all I have described to you the rent is only fifteen dollars a month?"

The new apartment was only a short distance from Peshine and Clinton Avenues, but the Halevys felt the move to Marie Place represented a move from the inner city to the suburbs. The adjustment to their new environment was minimal.

Shimon did, however, initiate a slow changing of his synagogue allegiance. Jews were moving from the Prince Street area into the South Ward, and their synagogues were ultimately to follow them. Shimon no longer felt exclusively drawn to his Morton Street congregation, but it remained his primary *shul* for some time.

Kalman thought the new home was fancy, but it made little difference to him; he was rarely home to enjoy it. Joshua initially complained about the move, regretting the friends and activities he left behind on Peshine Avenue. Marie Place initially seemed dull by comparison. He also had to switch schools again, this time to the Peshine Avenue School.

As Joshua walked to school on his first day, he received a warning from a neighbor.

"You're new here, aren't you?" the boy asked. "Well you had better get off the sidewalk."

"Why?"

"Because that's Kowalsky over there," the boy explained, pointing a hesitant finger ahead. "And he doesn't allow anybody on the sidewalk when he walks to school."

"That's nuts!" Joshua responded. Not wanting to be late for his first day in school, Joshua hurried on without pausing to find out more.

The next day, Joshua saw the feared Kowalsky again and decided to test his no-trespass policy. He walked directly behind him on the sidewalk, while the other kids either walked in the street or on the curb. They glanced apprehensively at Joshua as he edged closer to Kowalsky.

It took Kowalsky a few minutes to realize he was on the verge of a turf war. Suddenly, he turned around. "Nobody walks on the sidewalk when I'm around," he snarled at Joshua. "Didn't you hear about that?"

"Sure, I heard about it," Joshua retorted calmly, "but I think it's ridiculous. You don't own the sidewalk. You'll have to get me off if you want it for yourself."

"That will be easy," Kowalsky boasted. "But a fight right now would mess up our day. How about three-fifteen?"

"All right," Joshua agreed. "Where will it be?"

"On Jelliff and Meeker in the empty lot. That's where we have all our fights."

The news spread quickly among the students.

"Did you hear that? The new kid, Joshua, is going to fight Kowalsky," one boy exclaimed. "I guess he must have rocks in his head."

"Well, he never heard of Harry Kowalsky. I'll bet you a dozen immies Harry wins," another boy wagered.

By three-fifteen, a large crowd had gathered by the lot. Even some teachers came to watch the spectacle.

Joshua and Kowalsky were almost evenly matched in height and weight, though Joshua was a little heavier. By the time they entered the lot, the crowd had formed a circle around them. Without comment, the two started to fight.

Joshua knew if he could deliver a strong right-hand punch, he had a chance to win. But he couldn't connect. Kowalsky was too fast. He kept dancing around Joshua, punching away at every opportunity. Some of the blows hurt Joshua terribly, but he wouldn't give up. He continued charging Kowalsky.

One of the playground teachers finally stopped the fight. "Kowalsky wins," he decided, ceremoniously raising the victor's right hand. "But Joshua doesn't know when to quit. You guys better hold him back."

The feisty Joshua was still trying to charge his opponent, who wanted to congratulate him. Joshua finally realized the fight was over and started to grin at Kowalsky. Harry Kowalsky walked over to Joshua and put his arm around his shoulder.

"From now on, only two people can walk on the sidewalk when I'm around—me and Joshua," Kowalsky pompously declared.

Faige was alarmed at seeing Joshua's battered and bruised face when he returned home that afternoon. She knew that something more than a standard school brawl had occurred.

"What happened to you?" she demanded.

"Harry Kowalsky beat me up," Joshua replied candidly.

"Harry *who*?" Faige gaped with astonishment.

"Harry Kowalsky," Joshua repeated. "But it's all right, we're friends now."

His father laughed when he heard. "Well, it looks as if Kowalsky finally got his revenge," he said. "But he had to wait for the next generation."

# CHAPTER 25

★

*B*arely a year after the Halevys moved into their home on Marie Place, Faige received an all-too-familiar request. "I'm afraid you're going to have to move, Mrs. Halevy," her landlord said.

Faige looked at him in astonishment. "But, Mr. Sawyer, why should we have to move? We've barely been here a year."

"I'm sorry, Mrs. Halevy," he answered sympathetically. "There is nothing I can do. The house has been sold, and the new owner wants your apartment for himself. Don't take it personally. These things happen. You should have guessed that something was wrong when you moved in. Your rent was much too low. This was an estate house, and the heirs didn't care what the rent was as long as somebody lived here."

"Maybe I could pay a little more rent," Faige suggested.

"The new owner doesn't want higher rents," Mr. Sawyer replied. "He wants the apartment. He bought this house for himself and his married daughter. From what I understand, you people have moved often in the past. Why should you be so upset about it now?"

"Because we like the neighborhood," Faige answered, obviously distressed. "We don't want to move. This will upset my family very much."

Mr. Sawyer felt sorry for Faige. "What you should do is look for another apartment before you tell them about the move," he counseled. "Then you can tell them that you have to move from here, but you have another place to go to. There is an apartment available at 66 Watson Avenue. You might want to rent it."

"Where is Watson Avenue?"

"It's only two short blocks from here. The neighborhood is almost the same, just a little more commercial. The children would go to the same school."

"What does the apartment look like?" Faige asked cautiously.

"It's nice," he said. "It's part of a four-apartment house. The first floor is taken by stores, and the apartment is on the top floor, so you would be away from all the noise. The rooms are twice the size you have here, and the back yard is enormous. You should go right over there now before you tell your husband."

That evening Faige told Shimon about the move. "I think Mr. Sawyer is right about 66 Watson," she said. "The rooms are large, and the property is huge. And the rent is only eighteen dollars a month. I think we ought to take it."

"We probably don't have much of an alternative," Shimon answered. "Why don't you go over there tomorrow and give a deposit?"

"I already have," Faige answered. She hesitated somewhat before speaking further. "Shimon, dear, now that we've settled this matter, something else is going on that I don't think you are aware of."

"What's that?" Shimon wondered.

"Kalman heard from Martin Gross that your sister-in-law Shirley is pregnant," Faige said. "Did you know anything about that?"

"Here we go again," Shimon said, visibly upset. "If I had known anything about this, you would have, too."

"I can't believe it!" Faige exclaimed. "You see him every day, and the man doesn't tell his own brother that his wife is expecting. That goes against every rule of family conduct I have ever known. Imagine, we had to hear about it from Jersey City!"

Two weeks before his wife gave birth to a baby girl, Jacob casually told Shimon, while the latter was fashioning egg cartons, about the now imminent event. Shimon looked up fleetingly from his work, said *"Mazel tov"* and returned to his cardboard.

Shortly after Jacob and Shirley gave birth to a baby girl, the Halevys moved to 66 Watson Avenue. Despite the initial standard disorientation, the move turned out to be a positive one. Although Shimon and Kalman felt neutral about their new address, Faige enjoyed the large, airy rooms, while Leah and Moshe luxuriated in their spacious back yard. And Joshua was only a stone's throw from the playground.

After they moved, the *Shabbos* afternoon get-togethers with the Kagans and Ehrenses ended. The number of children between them tended to make meetings unmanageable, and none of them lived close by any more.

Mordechai Ehrens, who still worked as a *shochet*, was hired to serve as cantor of the Schley Street Shul and rented an apartment closer to his new workplace. Yosef Kagan evidenced his rising wealth by buying a one-family house on Wilber Avenue between Elizabeth Avenue and Bergen Street. But the three families remained friends, and Shimon and Faige saw them the following year at Joshua's *bar-mitzvah* in July.

Joshua performed almost all the *chazan's* roles that *Shabbos*, as well as the *haftorah* reading. It was a more extended assignment than most boys undertook, but Joshua's voice easily took control of the services. He felt little nervousness and boomed out each word clearly and accurately.

For a teacher, Shimon had contacted Nechemiah Mendelson, an older son of a local orthodox rabbi, who in turned referred Joshua to Chaim, the youngest Mendelson. Chaim was a bare six months older than his student, Joshua. He was only twelve when he taught himself his own *bar-mitzvah* material and tutored Joshua at the same time.

Chaim and Joshua quickly became friends. Joshua felt an affinity for his Orthodox friend that he didn't share with other boys at school. Besides the time they spent during the week, Joshua frequently joined Chaim's family on *Shabbos*. Shimon and Faige were pleased with their son's new friendship, though they thought it strange that Joshua preferred singing at the Mendelson's *Shabbos* table on Saturday afternoons to playing ball with his friends.

The two boys spent hours after their tutoring sessions discussing everything from shooting marbles to upcoming holidays. Chaim told Joshua all about the different customs his family observed, and Joshua wondered why his family didn't keep the same things.

"Papa," Joshua said, approaching his father after one such session in the spring. "Why are you going to work on the second day of *Pesach*? Chaim told me that it's a holiday just like the first day. His father never works on *Pesach*."

Shimon looked at his son in wonder. "Well, his father is a rabbi," he replied a little hesitantly. "His job is to stay at home or at *shul* on *Yom Tov*. My job is different. I never go to work on the first day of *Pesach*, but I can't take off two days. I don't have a choice."

Joshua shrugged his shoulders. His father's answer made sense to him. A job is a job. Still, he felt that if Chaim's father had not been a rabbi, he would have stayed home on the second day of *Yom Tov* anyhow.

When the day of Joshua's *bar-mitzvah* finally arrived, Shimon and Faige were stocked for an onslaught of guests. Shirley had helped Faige the previous week with her cooking and baking. But it was a very hot summer day, and many guests opted not to venture into the stifling Watson Avenue apartment. They chose to go to the park, and others decided to leave early.

"I hope Joshua won't be disappointed," Shirley said consolingly to Faige.

"Disappointed? Why should he be disappointed?" Faige snapped back. "We made a nice party. If people are selfish and prefer their own comforts to a party celebrating a *bar-mitzvah*, then that's their problem."

Kalman, who was thoroughly enjoying his weekend free from work, spotted Joshua wandering around the kitchen. "Where are your friends?" he asked him.

"They were here for a short while but then decided to go to the park."

"Are you upset?" Kalman asked.

"Nope," Joshua asserted evenly. "I got a suit with my first pair of long pants. Uncle Jacob and Aunt Shirley gave me a watch, and the Kagans gave me a pen and pencil set. I get to keep the presents, but Mom and Pop take the money."

A week after his party, Joshua officially began his summer vacation by joining a wrestling team at the playground. He met a black boy there his age. The boy's name was John Booie, and he and his brother Robert became Joshua's regular companions.

"I'm having trouble on the wrestling team," John confessed to Joshua one day at the playground.

"What's the matter?" Joshua asked.

"Well, I'm not getting many matches."

"Have you talked to the coaches about it yet?" Joshua suggested.

"Oh sure, but they don't want to tell me the truth," John answered.

Joshua looked confused. "What do you mean?"

"Well, I don't think the white boys want to wrestle with a Negro," John intimated.

"Could be," Joshua answered, nonplussed. "But I don't understand it. I would wrestle with you."

"Would you?" John asked eagerly.

Joshua nodded his head. Within two weeks of joining, having barely learned the mat rules and the more immobilizing holds, he was pitted against John Booie.

The small gym where the wrestling matches were held was jammed. The match had excited the playground denizens, who bet clamorously on the outcome. Even Joshua's basketball team rescheduled its game so that they could attend.

It took John Booie almost all of the allotted fifteen minutes to pin Joshua's shoulders to the mat. For a while, when Joshua had John in a full nelson, he began to feel that he might even win. But John was able to break away and immediately jumped Joshua to make his winning move.

As the audience cheered John, an onlooker bent his head to Joshua. "How did it feel to have a Negro sweat over you?" he asked.

The two wrestlers lunged for the antagonist, but the coaches intervened.

Later that day, John again surprised Joshua. "You know why we get along so well together, don't you?" he asked.

"No," Joshua answered. "How should I know?"

"We're both Jewish," John disclosed.

"What?" Joshua exclaimed, not sure if his friend was jesting.

"It's true," John said. "My mother converted when she came up North."

"I've never seen you in the synagogue," Joshua pointed out quickly.

"I've been there many times," John answered. "But I always stay in the back. You never noticed. You're too busy with your friends in the front."

"Well, I'll be darned," Joshua managed, absolutely astonished.

John leaned over towards Joshua. "There is something you can do for me, Joshua," he began.

"What's that?"

"I have never seen a Torah up close," he said. "Can you manage that one for me?"

Joshua thought for a moment before he replied. "Yes, I suppose I can."

"You can?" John asked excitedly. "How?"

"Well, now it's early afternoon," Joshua said, glancing at his watch, "so nobody will be in the *shul*. I can take you in, put a Torah on the *bimah* and let you see it."

"How will we get in?" John asked.

"The door is open almost all the time," Joshua guaranteed, "and Mr. Moskowitz sits in front of it saying psalms. He's always there. Mr. Moskowitz will let you in if you're with me."

"Can Robert come, too?" John asked eagerly. "He's also Jewish, you know."

Joshua nodded his head, and the three headed to *shul*. Mr. Moskowitz seemed slightly surprised at the three entering the synagogue, but he nodded amiably to Joshua.

"I want to show them something," Joshua explained.

He went to the *aron*, removed a *sefer Torah* and brought it to the *bimah*. Holding it tightly in his arms, he gently lowered it onto the *bimah*. Then he untied the *gartel's* knot and showed the awed boys the parchment. John and Robert looked hesitantly at Joshua and then gingerly touched the velvet covering. Joshua waited patiently until the two black boys nodded to him. Then he rewrapped the *sefer Torah* and carefully put it back.

In August of that summer, Joshua took on his first regular job. A man had come around the playground looking for someone to help him deliver pinball machines to candy stores. The work was slated for five days a week from eight in the morning to one in the afternoon, and the pay was one dollar a day.

Joshua took on the job mainly to help out his parents at home, though they hadn't asked him to get a job. He also wanted to alleviate what he considered his embarrassing plight of having to borrow money at the local grocery store.

The United Grocery Store, on the corner of Watson and Belmont Avenues, was operated by a kind and dignified gentile. His name was Mr. Smith. Faige regularly kept an account at the store, which she carefully balanced each pay day. When the end of the week came, however, Faige frequently did not have enough money to do her *Shabbos* shopping. She sent Joshua to Mr. Smith to borrow three or five dollars and charge it to her account. Mr. Smith, who empathized with her financial tribulations, readily loaned the money with no detectable rancor or anger. Still, Joshua was embarrassed and resentful about having to ask for money. It was the only time he ever felt poor.

By all objective standards, the household was indeed poor. Yet none of its members felt that way. Their home always evinced the aromatic redolence of freshly cooked and baked foods. They even owned one of the first household refrigerators in the neighborhood, a Gibson, for which Faige had obligated herself to pay five dollars a month for two years. And they owned a quality radio set contained within its own floor cabinet.

Once the fall began, Joshua gave up his job. It was his last year of junior high, and unlike Kalman, Joshua was determined to finish school. His parents knew Joshua enjoyed school, and they didn't pressure him to abandon his studies to help the family.

Joshua graduated from junior high in January of 1935, the Peshine Avenue School having bi-annual graduations in January and June. Shimon and Faige beamed with pride at the graduation. To them, this milestone imparted meaning to so many of the ordeals they had gone through since they moved to America. And they knew Joshua would have never gotten so far in Skalat.

# CHAPTER 26

★

$\mathcal{Y}$osef Kagan, already known as the tuna fish king, met Shimon in *shul* one *Shabbos* shortly after *Purim*. After *davening*, he pulled Shimon aside. "Did you hear what's going on with your brother's business?"

Shimon's blank face revealed that he hadn't.

Yosef looked exasperated. "I can't believe you work for your brother's business, and you know nothing about the talk that is all over town. The story is that Mr. Fischer is pulling in his IOU's on Jacob's business."

"Jacob owes him money?" Shimon asked.

"No. I don't think it's money," Yosef continued. "Or certainly it can't be very much money. There's more to it than that. Remember, Fischer gave Jacob his first job as a dairy salesman. They've been business associates for years. It was Fischer who talked Jacob into going into his own business when he opened the Uco Food Corporation."

Shimon looked confused. "So, what has changed?"

"Well, Uco never took off," Yosef explained. "It's hard to build a nationwide food business even with all the new inventions out. Also, the Depression is hurting him. Fischer is finding himself loaded down with a huge plant on Freilynghuysen Avenue that is half-empty. That's hard to explain to investors."

"What does it have to do with Jacob?" Shimon questioned his friend.

"I think Fischer talked Jacob into joining Uco," Yosef divulged, watching Shimon for his reaction. "He probably told him that the growth potential is greater than with his own firm. I think Jacob made a mistake. The Depression is hard on all of us, but if he sells out now he could be left with nothing. But knowing you and your brother, I'm not surprised if Jacob will do it. He insists on being loyal even to his own detriment."

Yosef was right. Within a week, Jacob called together all his employees and substantiated the rumor. He assured them he would be in charge of the butter and egg department of Uco, and that he planned no changes in the number of employees or their salaries.

To Shimon, he added privately, "It makes absolutely no difference to you. Wherever I go, you'll come with me. I'll see to it you always have a job."

Faige received the news with a kind of vindicating laugh. "Now he's a worker just like you are," she said.

"Yes, but he's the boss," Shimon answered, trying hard to rationalize Jacob's decision. "They say he makes a hundred dollars a week."

"That may be," Faige interrupted, "but he doesn't own a business any longer. I sometimes think we were better off when you were in the coal business. At least, we hoped that things could be better. And what about your salary? Did he at least ask for a higher salary for you at Uco?"

Shimon looked down at the floor. "How could he ask for a

raise for me? It's not his business any more."

Faige was incensed. "Why don't you face the facts and stop apologizing for your brother? Sure, he's helped us. Any brother would. But he's just plain selfish. He never thinks of helping his struggling brother's family by giving him a well-deserved raise, even if it would only be two dollars! Don't justify him to me. I see right through him."

Faige's angry words echoed Shimon's private thoughts, though he was loathe to think of his brother as selfish. He knew Jacob had had a hard life growing up on his own and was sure he would have acted differently if he hadn't left home by himself at the tender age of thirteen. Still, when Thursday came around every week and he had to buy fish and chicken for *Shabbos* on credit, he was resentful.

But Shimon did not want to argue with Faige and instead changed the subject. "It looks like you'll be seeing Jacob every morning when the company moves."

"How come?"

"He'll be picking me up in the mornings to go to work," Shimon explained. "So, I suppose he'll come up for coffee."

"Lucky me," Faige said.

Jacob's early morning visits proved to be disastrous. At the time, his two children, Robert and Bernice, were ill with the highly contagious scarlet fever. Jacob did not know that he, too, was a carrier.

Leah was the first to become sick, and the house went under a limited quarantine. A big red notice was placed on the front door of 66 Watson Avenue warning the public that there was a case of scarlet fever on the third floor. Joshua and Moshe, who was eight years old at the time, were considered at risk and had to leave their home.

No one with young children wanted to shelter the brothers. Because Jacob's house still had two weeks to go before its own quarantine was repealed, Jacob was barred from taking his nephews in. Shimon ended up making an interim arrangement with Aaron and Sarah Zwillman, whom he knew from *shul.*

The Zwillmans owned a large, one-family house on the corner of Meeker and Elizabeth Avenues, opposite Weequahic Park. They lived there alone, but it was rumored that their son, Longy, who was reputed to be a bootlegger, used the house as a conference center for his workers.

When Joshua and Moshe arrived at the house, they stood on the steps of the porch and looked up at the formidable looking knocker on the door. Moshe held his small suitcase in one hand and squeezed Joshua's hand with the other.

"Why can't we just stay at home?" he asked in a small voice. "We could sleep in the back yard."

"Don't be silly," Joshua replied. "It's cold outside. And we don't have much choice. We can't stay in our house if we want to go to school. You better like it here. Mom says we may be here for two or three weeks."

Moshe whimpered. "I want to go home. Can't I just go home and say good-bye to Mama one more time?"

"No," Joshua answered firmly. "That's the whole idea of quarantine. We can't go into our house. The most we can do is go into the backyard and call Mom out to the porch. That's the only way we can see her for the next couple of weeks."

Now Moshe was on the verge of tears.

"You better not cry," Joshua warned. "Longy Zwillman is a gangster."

Moshe could not contain himself any longer. He dropped his suitcase and began to sob.

Joshua knew he had gone too far. He set down his own suitcase and gave his brother a hug. "Don't worry," he said consolingly as he wiped away Moshe's tears. "I'll be with you." Then he reached up and knocked on the door.

"Come in," a gruff voice called out.

Joshua and Moshe let themselves in and timidly walked ahead into what they thought was the kitchen.

"Not that way," someone said. "Come up the stairs."

Joshua and Moshe climbed up the stairs that led into a small sitting room. Aaron and Sarah were sitting at a table reading the newspaper.

"There are two beds in the attic," Sarah said, barely looking up from her paper.

Nothing else was said, and Joshua realized that he and his brother were dismissed. They continued into the attic. Queer folks, he thought. No wonder their son is a gangster.

Moshe spent two nights in the Zwillman house before he, too, contracted scarlet fever. The doctor, mindful of Faige's difficulties caring for two sick children, recommended Moshe be taken to Soho Isolation Hospital.

"You're not made of iron," the doctor advised. "You're already caring for your daughter twenty-four hours a day. Adding your son to your responsibilities could be too much. You could get sick yourself. Soho is an excellent facility, and I'm sure Moshe would be well taken care of."

Faige discussed the idea with Shimon that evening. "Leah reminds me so much of Neshe," Faige said softly, "though she should live for many more years than her sister. I'll never forget what I went through with her. Maybe I did something wrong then. Perhaps I can't take care of two very sick children. I am not sure Moshe would be better off in the hospital or at home. But I think I have to let them take him to the hospital."

The doctor was informed of the decision, and the ambulance arrived for Moshe that day. The attendants strapped a weeping boy to the cot and started to carry him down the stairs.

Suddenly, Faige gave out a shriek. "Stop! Bring him back!" she screamed. "I can't send Moshe to the hospital, where no one knows him. Bring him back! I'll take care of him right here."

Faige's decision extended the quarantine to a total of three weeks. Except for the last week, Joshua spent all his time at the Zwillmans. Once the quarantine had finally been lifted at his Uncle Jacob's house, a grateful Joshua headed there.

"I had my own isolation," Joshua told his uncle and aunt. "Once I went into that house in the afternoon, I didn't speak to anyone until the next day. I ended up reading, and I even did some homework."

"I'll bet that's a first," Jacob laughed.

"The worst part was our neighbors," Joshua continued, ignoring his uncle's remark. "Can you believe it? They complained to the Board of Health when I went up the stairs to get something from my mother. Most of the time I spoke to her from our backyard, but when I went up the stairs to hear her better, they complained. The Board of Health made me go to Washington Street to take a blood test in order to prove that I wasn't a carrier."

Unlike his experience with the Zwillmans, Joshua thoroughly enjoyed his week with his uncle and aunt. Robert was the same age as Moshe, and Bernice was an adorable five-year-old. Joshua loved the children and got along well with them, so much so that his Aunt Shirley decided to use him as a paid baby-sitter.

Joshua returned home when the quarantine was lifted. But before he could even get resettled, his mother surprised him with some news. "We're going to have to move, you know," she said.

Joshua was startled. "Move? Why should we move? I've just come home."

"We can't live here any more," Faige said matter-of-factly. "Do you want to live with people who went running to the Board of Health when you came to the porch to see me? I don't. I can't wait to leave. You shouldn't have bad feelings against your neighbors, and if you do, you have to move."

"Where are we going to go this time, Mom?" Joshua asked.

"I don't know. When I know, I'll tell you," came a frank assurance.

Joshua cheered his mother with his bit of news. "I think I have a job, Mom," he told her.

"Good," she replied. "We could use some extra money. Where is it?"

"It's with Mrs. Grossman," Joshua said. "Do you remember Mr. Grossman, my friend Morty's father, who died a couple of months ago?"

Faige nodded, and Joshua continued. "The family has a house on Milford Avenue right near my school, and they operate a mail order business in contact lenses."

"What would you do for them?" Faige asked.

"Mrs. Grossman works the business alone now, and it's too much for her," Joshua explained. "Morty wants to be an engineer, so he goes to a technical high school in New York. Anyway, Morty is never home, and Mrs. Grossman asked me to work with her."

"How much will she pay you for your work?" Faige got down to business.

"The job is three afternoons a week, on Mondays, Wednesdays, and Thursdays, from around three-thirty in the afternoon to six-thirty. She'll pay me two dollars a day."

"That's better than nothing," Faige said.

Joshua enjoyed his job with the soft-spoken Mrs. Grossman. The Grossman basement had been turned into a large room for warehousing the lenses. A large table stood in the middle of the room supporting cartons, wrapping paper, scissors and tape. It was Joshua's job to fill as many orders as he could and prepare a list of those lenses that were out of stock.

Joshua marvelled at the complexity and variety of the many

different permutations of lens prescriptions. He also liked working with Mrs. Grossman, a small, thin woman with a strong German accent.

Joshua handed over the money he earned to his parents, and they let him keep some pocket money for himself. He bought his first big-ticket item, a used bicycle, which cost him three dollars. His immediate incentive was pedaling to Weequahic Park on Sundays to play tennis with Chaim.

Soon, Joshua had a more commercial use in mind for his bicycle. He approached Morty one weekend. "How can I carry eggs on my bicycle without breaking them?"

"Why would you want to carry eggs on your bicycle?" Morty asked.

"Well, the Uco Food Company is only around fifteen minutes away from home by bike," Joshua explained. "That's where my father and uncle work. I want to buy eggs from them and sell them door to door using my bicycle."

"That's a real challenge," Morty said, scratching his head. But he took to the idea and started at once to help Joshua put his plan into action.

It took the boys two weeks to finalize their plan. First, they found an old baby carriage with a padded body. They changed the axles and mounted small balloon tires. Then they installed automobile shock absorbers between the wheels and the carriage bottom. Morty obtained two long steel bars, which he used to bolt the trailer to the frame of the bicycle. Joshua then sanded and painted the bike and trailer in jet black.

The bicycle worked perfectly. Unfortunately, Joshua never got to use it. During the year he worked at the Grossmans, he had no time to canvass customers, and by the summer of his sophomore year, he accepted a job at a general store on Prince Street. This part-time job after school consisted of a forty-plus-hour work week, for which Joshua earned twelve dollars. He was earning six dollars a week less than his father and doing it part-time.

Though Faige had been looking actively for a new apartment since the scarlet fever episode, she did not find one until the spring of 1936. They moved to 323 Peshine Avenue, a street bordered by Hawthorne Avenue and West Runyon Street.

Kalman considered the address "fancy," though he was rarely home to enjoy it. The building, which housed their apartment, was a three-floor, twelve-family brick apartment. The Halevys occupied three bedrooms on the third floor. A second cousin to Shimon, also named Halevy, lived on the first floor.

The neighborhood was dominated by Jewish lower-middle class residents, many of whom Faige had known before she moved onto the street. She was very pleased with their new location, while once again Shimon was utterly neutral. Jacob still picked him up every morning to go to work, and Mendelson's *shul* on Bergen Street was just a little closer.

The move meant little to Joshua or to Leah, who was now called Lila. Lila was ten years old, entering the sixth grade that September. She was a straight honor student and was allowed to stay at the Peshine Avenue School for her junior high school years.

But for nine-year-old Moshe, now known as Morris, the move was devastating. He was forced to transfer from the smaller Peshine Avenue School where he, Joshua and Lila were well-known, to a larger and more impersonal one. His Jewish education also suffered. He had to leave Temple Bnai Abraham and register in the loosely-organized school operated by Rabbi Mendelson and his children. Though they were well-intentioned, the rabbi's sons and daughters who taught in the Hebrew school were not professionals, and Morris suffered from their complete incompetence.

# CHAPTER 27

★

Five years after Kalman had begun his laborious job for his cousin Martin Gross, Jacob came to pay him a visit. The doorbell rang on a Sunday afternoon, as Kalman lay exhausted on the couch, having just returned home.

Jacob came directly to the point. "A few years ago," he began, "I helped Lew Isaacson get a job with the White Rose Tea Company. His father is one of my customers, and I was glad I could help his son get into a good company. Lew is doing very well and just got a promotion. He has become the Northeastern Sales Manager and will be in charge of all the White Rose salesmen in this area."

Kalman and his parents listened to Jacob, wondering what this had to do with them.

"Well, Lew's old job is now open," Jacob explained, "and I've recommended Ken for the position. You'll have to go for an interview, but I think it's yours. It pays twenty-five dollars a week plus bonuses. They always have contests for salesmen who make the most sales. Lew wants you to start in a week, so that's all the notice that you can give to Martin. He'll have to understand, and I'm sure he wants what's best for you."

Jacob sat back on the couch, watching the effects of his words sink into his eager audience.

Kalman spoke first. "Do you mean I'm finally going to leave Jersey City?" he asked disbelievingly.

"Well, we knew when you first started to work there the job would only be a stepping stone to something better," Jacob replied. "Martin tells me you've learned the grocery business very well. I'm sure you'll be successful with the White Rose Company. It's a good company, and Lew's a good man."

Faige could not contain her enthusiasm. "Thank Heaven, the nightmare is over," she exulted, knowing how her son had suffered silently for his family. "Kalman can start living normally."

Shimon watched the scene and glowed, relishing the rare opportunity of celebrating his brother's kindness. He nodded knowingly at Faige, to make sure she had acknowledged it, too.

Kalman's new job boosted his morale and his family's funds. He also no longer felt as if he was the only child responsible for helping out. Joshua's part-time job brought in extra cash, and even Lila at eleven and Morris at ten began to look for part-time work. Lila found a position with a lumber company as assistant to the bookkeeper, and Morris took a job delivering telegrams for Western Union by bicycle.

In spite of Joshua's part-time jobs, he still was able to maintain average grades and take on extracurricular activities. He was a member of the Glee Club, where he became a standard soloist at almost all the group's public performances, and he joined the Debating Club. He was also appointed to the All-State Chorus, which was rehearsing the Chorale from Beethoven's Ninth Symphony when Joshua joined. The music was to be played the following summer in an outdoor concert at Bloomfield High School Stadium and was to be conducted by the world-famous Arturo Toscanini.

When he started rehearsing for the concert, Joshua faced a dilemma. The practice sessions were held at the Mosque Theater on Broad Street on Saturday mornings, which was when he usually accompanied Lila and Morris to the synagogue. They preferred to go to the local Conservative synagogue, where there were more youngsters, than to Rabbi Mendelson's *shul* with their father. Shimon, whose observance was more out of habit than conviction, had come to terms with having his children attend Conservative services while he himself attended Orthodox services. Joshua started attending the rehearsals, but very soon he began to feel guilty.

He told his parents that he was going to quit the rehearsals. "Kalman never goes with Lila and Morris," Joshua reasoned. "If I stop going now, how long do you think it will be before they stop going to synagogue altogether?"

Faige was taken aback at her son's efflorescence of religious piety.

"But what about when you have to work on Saturdays?" she asked. "What do you do then?"

"That's different, Mom," Joshua answered. "I have to work on Saturdays, but I don't have to go to practice. I love being in the chorus, but I don't feel comfortable with the Saturday sessions."

Joshua told the directors of the chorus about his problem and found them hearteningly understanding. One of them even told him he would make sure Joshua was hired as an usher. "That way, you'll still be part of the production, and you won't have to pay to see the concert."

That winter, Jacob informed Shimon and Faige that he had sold his property on Tenth Street and Avon Avenue. "All those garages that I used for the butter and egg company needed too much maintenance."

"Where are you going to live now?" Faige asked.

"Well, we didn't buy anything yet because we're not sure where we want to be," Jacob allowed. "We've rented an apartment on Pomona Avenue in the Weequahic section. Their schools are better, and we'll see how we like living there before we buy a house." He paused for a moment. "Also, Shirley is pregnant."

"*Mazel tov!*" Shimon and Faige exclaimed together, more delighted at having been told than at the news itself.

In the spring of 1937, a few months after Jacob's announcement, Shirley was found dead on the kitchen floor of their apartment. She had bled to death. Jacob had tried unsuccessfully to reach her by telephone, inferred something was wrong and rushed home to discover the body.

Jacob was broken by tragedy. "How much can a man take?" he grieved. "First my mother when I was barely twelve years old and now my wife. It's impossible to live."

"Well, you'll have to find a way to live," Shimon reassured him. "Bernice is six years old, and Robert is ten. You have no choice but to live."

Within two years, in 1939, Jacob announced his intention to remarry. His intended, Betty Levine, had never been married before and was the sister-in-law of one of Newark's prominent doctors. Like Shirley, she was a native-born American and lived a markedly different life from Shimon and Faige. Yet, she got along well with Faige, and the two brothers maintained the same relationship as they had before.

That same year, Joshua graduated from high school. His graduation took place in January at the South Side High School auditorium, and the entire Halevy family attended. They all watched proudly as Joshua walked down the aisle in his cap and gown and stepped onto the stage to receive his diploma. Then they applauded wildly when Joshua returned to the stage later to receive his gold debating medal.

The graduating classes of 1939 would have little time for celebration. Abroad, a war was brewing that looked more and more likely to include the United States. Still, as Joshua and his classmates accepted their diplomas, the Depression was a much more proximate concern. Jobs were still very scarce, even though some economists had declared that the end of the great downturn was now at hand.

Joshua's latest part-time job was in a haberdashery on Prince Street. Before graduation, however, it had started to wind down until it was completely eliminated. This left Joshua nervous about finding new work and anxious not to disappoint his family.

Joshua realized that his parents were becoming increasingly dependent on his salary. Kalman, now twenty-seven years old, was doing very well with the White Rose Tea Company. He had quickly become one of the firm's most productive salesmen and consistently won awards offered for top sales performance. He had also been dating Mildred Karp and announced his intention to marry that August.

While joyous and excited about the news, Faige was worried about losing Kalman's income. Would Joshua be able to take over Kalman's share of the expenses?

While Joshua looked for a job, he surprised his parents with some novel plans. "Tonight I'm going to register at Newark Junior College," he told his mother over breakfast.

Faige looked incredulous. "Whatever for?"

"I'm going to take a philosophy course at night," Joshua said. "I might as well start night college right away. That's the only way I'm going to get anywhere."

"What about a job?" Shimon asked.

"I've been looking," Joshua answered. "It's not that easy.

But I don't want to waste my time doing nothing. That's why I'm taking this class."

Shimon was not impressed. "I don't see how philosophy is going to help you get a job," he said.

Shimon spoke to Jacob about Joshua the very next day. "Isn't there anything you can do for him?" he asked timidly.

Jacob was not encouraging. "You know, Joshua isn't at all like Ken," he said. "When it came to Ken, I never doubted he belonged in the grocery business. But Joshua is different. He graduated high school, and he loved school, too. He's even religious to a certain extent. He's the only boy I know his age who still puts on *tefillin*. It's not going to be as easy to find him a job as it was for Ken."

"Isn't there something you can do?" Shimon repeated his request.

Jacob scratched his head in thought. "I couldn't bring him into Uco even if there was an opening. The office politics are prohibitive. I have two experienced dairymen there already, and it would be difficult to justify a third, especially my nephew."

"Is there another grocery store you know of?" Faige asked.

"I can probably bring him into the Giant Tiger Market," Jacob concluded, "but only as an extra helper on weekends. I think that would be the best solution for everyone."

Shimon was not satisfied with a part-time job for his son, but he did not complain to his brother. He thanked Jacob and told him that he hoped it would work out.

Before Shimon left, Jacob suddenly had an idea. "I just thought of something. Joshua could work as a waiter at the Mountain Lake Hotel. I know the people there. That would take care of part of the spring and the summer, and by that time, maybe things will loosen up a little bit."

Joshua liked both parts of Jacob's plan. Faige liked neither. "If he was really interested in securing a full-time job for you, he could have," she said. "He has plenty of connections. He just doesn't care enough."

Shimon did not respond to Faige's accusation, and Joshua wisely ignored it. He was eager to start any job he could get, and the job as a waiter in a mountain hotel in particular appealed to him.

The following weekend, Joshua began work at the Giant Tiger. The Giant Tiger operation represented an attempt by the food wholesalers to retail their products to the general public. It was also the start of the modern supermarket. The market was a huge building with little more than a ceiling and walls. Its dirt floor was dotted with sawdust in some areas to aid walking. There were many separate concessions, sold off by the operators.

Joshua was put in charge of the dairy department for Uco. He loved the excitement and the ubiquitous throngs of people waiting to be helped. Joshua took to his task enthusiastically, doing his work even before he was told. Although his co-workers suspected he was a mere nepotist's figurehead, as Jacob had predicted, they came to trust him after a while and regard him as just another worker. And at twelve dollars a week for three days' work, his compensation was proportionately richer than his father's.

As Memorial Day approached, Joshua made plans to go to Ellenville, New York, to start his summer job. The Mountain Lake Hotel had originally been owned by a first cousin to Shimon and Jacob. It had been known as Halevy and Heller's Mountain Lake Hotel. Now the Hausman family from the grocery store on Elizabeth Avenue were the hotel's principal owners.

The hotel was run primarily by Frieda, an elderly aunt and widow of one of the original owners, and her second husband Abraham. It consisted of a main, three-story building with twenty rooms to a floor and bathrooms and showers at each end of the hall. The lobby was the living room of a separate house, which housed the family and some guests, and was attached to a large dining room.

Joshua loved the hotel grounds. They were relaxing, serene and beautiful. He loved looking out at the surrounding mountains and in the evening, the pristine sky all but delivered the stars into his hands.

Joshua was not as enamored of the hotel. He found many of the guests to be grossly demanding and unpleasant in their expectations from the small and overworked staff. He compared his duties to waiting on ten people at one time in the Giant Tiger Market. The trick was to make each person feel he was next and to smile a lot.

Joshua was told he could bring a friend with him to work the regular season in the summer. He had Chaim in mind.

"Chaim," Frieda tested the name on her tongue. "What kind of a boy uses his Hebrew name all of the time?"

"Well, he's a rabbi's son," Joshua started to explain.

"A rabbi's son," Frieda answered. "We don't need a rabbi's son here to tell us what to do."

"He's not that kind of a rabbi's son," Joshua clarified. "He's not interested in religion like his father is, and he certainly never tells anyone what to do."

"All right, I'll take your word for it," Frieda answered. "Now, here's how the job works. There is no pay from the hotel. We give you room and board, and you depend on tips for your salary. So the more people you take care of, the more tips you can make. If you and your friend work together, you can be the waiter in the children's dining room and a busboy in the main dining hall. Chaim can set your tables for you while you're serving the children. Then you'll come in to bus your own tables after they eat."

Chaim accepted the invitation eagerly, and the boys came

to work a few days before the fourth of July. Everything went as planned in terms of their work schedule. But the living conditions were terrible. They had to share their sleeping quarters with ten men of all ages and backgrounds in a barn, including two drunkards.

The dining room help usually worked twenty-hour days and got perhaps an hour off between lunch and dinner. But the food was not always available to the help. It was not unusual to serve an entire meal only to find that the cooks had run out of food. Chaim and Joshua began ordering extra portions during meals. They hid them in the serving tables and ate them later.

At the end of August, Joshua took a few days off to attend Kalman's wedding. Despite a burn on the right side of his face from spilled coffee and exhaustion from travelling back and forth, Joshua was gone only a few days. The work ethic ran deep in the Halevy family.

# CHAPTER 28

★

$\mathscr{S}$hortly after *Sukkos* of that year, Shimon and Faige learned that Rabbi Abraham Heschel from Skalat, the Kapichenitzer Rebbe, had arrived in America with most of his family and had settled on Henry Street in New York City. Shimon and Faige rushed to see them and between tears learned of the horrors that had already begun to plague the Jews in Eastern Europe. Shimon and Faige shuddered as they thought of their relatives back in Skalat and silently acknowledged the significance of their move two decades before.

Shmuel Hakatan and his family had also emigrated to America with Rabbi Heschel. Shimon was delighted to greet his old friend and remembered how he had been the first man to greet him on his return to Skalat in 1920.

Shmuel brought with him a parcel from Zvi Hersh. Shimon gingerly opened up the brown paper bag and pulled out a huge, beautiful *tallis*, crowned with a majestic silver *atarah*. The entire family marvelled at this remembrance from their patriarch, and

Shimon was to wear the *tallis* proudly for the rest of his life.

That fall, when Joshua began his new job, he learned that the anti-semitism that was raging in Europe had seeped into New Jersey as well. He found his job by answering a newspaper ad for a dairy manager in a supermarket concession. Impressed with his Giant Tiger experience, the interviewer hired him. His job was to steward the dairy department at the Irvington branch of the King Supermarket chain, a chain which had recently expanded.

Joshua's boss was Mr. Fryer, a tall, thin man with a sardonic demeanor. Joshua cautiously followed Mr. Fryer around as he showed him about the store, making painstaking efforts to smile and nod at him at every opportunity.

"Joshua—that's an odd name—will run the dairy counter for you," Mr. Fryer introduced him to the other employees. "He seems to be experienced, so there shouldn't be any problems. If he needs any help at peak sales times and you can spare somebody, you'll send him over. If not, Joshua will have to manage."

Then Mr. Fryer showed Joshua into his office. "I told you about the store hours, didn't I?" he asked impassively. "Mondays to Wednesdays from eight am to eight pm. Thursdays to Saturdays the store is open until ten. Your pay is twenty-three dollars a week. Tom is your boss when I'm not around. Any questions?"

"No," Joshua answered. "I think I know what you want done, and I'll do it."

"Good," said Mr. Fryer without even a hint of a smile. He turned to Tom, who had just stepped into the office. "He can start right away, can't he, Tom?"

"Absolutely," was the instant reply. "I've been hurting ever since you fired Kurt."

Mr. Fryer glared at Tom. Evidently, he didn't want a new employee to know people got fired.

Everything went well with Joshua the first few weeks, but undercurrents of talk lapped against his reputation. Irvington was predominantly German. A Jewish manager of the dairy counter was considered an affront.

"But how do they know you are Jewish?" Chaim asked Joshua soon after he began at King.

"I don't know," Joshua answered. "I wouldn't deny being Jewish if anyone asked me, but nobody has. I don't treat anyone differently. Everything is always neat and clean, and I try to serve customers as best I can. But no matter how nice I am to them, they don't reciprocate, especially this anti-semite, Mr. Karr. He stands to one side of the counter glaring at me while I'm waiting on the people ahead of him. It's like he's waiting for something to happen."

A few weeks later, something did.

Chaim listened intently as Joshua related the episode. "Last week when it came to Mr. Karr's turn, I asked how I could help him. He said, 'It's about time you waited on me. I guess you must be through taking care of your Jewish friends.'"

Chaim looked shocked. "What did you say to him?"

"First, I didn't say anything. I felt like jumping over the counter and giving him a punch. But of course, I didn't. Instead, I said, 'I'm ready for you now, sir. What can I get for you?'"

"Good for you, Joshua," Chaim said supportively.

"That's not the end of it," Joshua continued. "A couple of days later, Karr came back and wanted to buy some cigarettes. We sell a lot of them at the counter. Just the day before, Fryer had ordered me to cut back on the free matches we give out. He told me that from then on I was to give five books a carton instead of the whole box of matches, which has around twenty packs. Mr. Karr buys three cartons a week. Can you imagine his reaction when I gave him fifteen books of matches?"

"It must have been exciting," Chaim said dryly.

"It was," Joshua affirmed. "You could hear Karr scream at the other end of the store. He yelled, 'You cheap Jew, do you think I'm going to let you get away with that? You can keep your cigarettes, and I'm going to tell my friends not to buy them here any more. You're not going to get away with this.'"

"Did you say anything?" Chaim wanted to know.

"No," Joshua answered. "What could I say?"

That same week, the sale of carton cigarettes plunged from fifty cartons a week to five, and Joshua was fired. Fryer came to the store on a Saturday night an hour before closing time and told Joshua to check out his register. After he did, Fryer acknowledged to Joshua that he was through.

The self-possessed Joshua was shocked. It was the first time he had ever been fired, and he was shaken about having to fling the new crisis at his parents.

Shimon and Faige were not as disturbed by Joshua's tale. In spite of it all, America was *galus*, too.

"But what now?" Faige asked.

Jacob, who had been visiting at the time, had an answer. "I'm going to send him to a market in East Orange. There are two young fellows who are starting up from nothing, and they need some help. It's only temporary, but we'll keep going this way until something good breaks our way."

"It's all right with me," Joshua said.

That evening, Faige surprised her family. "I'm afraid we're going to have to move again."

"Move again?" Joshua groused. "We like it here. This is the nicest place we ever had. Why do we have to move?"

"Because the rent is too expensive," Faige answered. "With Kalman gone, we can't take a chance of not being able to pay the rent. Once you have a steady job, things will be different. I found a nice place on Hillside Avenue and West Runyon Street.

The rooms are larger than we have here, and the landlord will paint before we move in."

"Oh no," Lila shuddered. "Here we go again."

"What do you mean, here we go again?" Faige charged in a rare spell of anger. "Are you missing anything? Do you lack anything? Well, you won't be missing anything over there either. You can go to South Side High School from there just as well as from here, and so can Moshe."

"But I wanted to go to Weequahic," Moshe complained.

"Do you hear that?" Faige retorted. "Only Weequahic High will do. I'm afraid you'll have to do without it."

Joshua's East Orange job was a breeze compared to his trials at Irvington. The emphasis was on work, not inter-ethnic conflicts. But his job did not last long. At the end of 1939, business began to run dry, and Joshua was out looking for work again.

He found employment as a temporary holiday employee with Bamberger's department store and was assigned to the men's clothing department. At the same time, he began taking evening courses at the Newark College of Engineering.

Joshua was busy from early morning till late at night. But he did not complain, especially since he loved his job.

"It's a pleasure," he told his mother. "Everything is so clean, not like a supermarket. I dress in a shirt and tie every day, and I feel good about myself."

Joshua was kept on months after the December rush, and his supervisor tried unsuccessfully to retain him for the Easter rush. But he had already obtained a spring job at Bond Clothes, almost directly across the street from Bamberger's. Joshua was successful at Bond's as well, and his boss and co-workers liked his easygoing style. But by the summer of 1940, the store returned to its normal schedule, and the extra staff was terminated.

Joshua once again found himself behind a dairy counter, this time at a supermarket in Kearny, New Jersey, courtesy of Uncle Jacob. The supermarket had been founded by the Uco company as part of the Giant Tiger operation, and Jacob had been in charge from its earliest beginnings. Joshua worked there for almost two years.

On Sunday, December 7, 1941, Joshua lay half-asleep on his living room couch, listening to the New York Philharmonic Orchestra play *Tristan and Isolde* on the radio. Bulletins interrupted the program, reporting the Japanese attack on Pearl Harbor. The news only half-stirred Joshua at first. When he finally realized what had happened, he ran around the empty apartment looking for someone to whom to talk.

The implications of American participation in the war dawned quickly on Joshua. Kalman was twenty-nine and too old for the approaching draft, while Morris at fourteen was too young. Only Joshua at twenty was vulnerable. But as the weeks turned into months, without any hint of a draft notice, Joshua and his parents pushed the thought out of their minds and concentrated on bringing in their weekly salary instead.

For Joshua, this meant being bounced around to a new job again. The principal partners of the Uco Food Corporation, where Jacob and Shimon worked, had severed their relationship and cast the company into bankruptcy. After a few chaotic weeks, one of the partners decided to buy Gude and Cole, a wholesale dairy company, and operate it as a family enterprise.

Jacob came into the enterprise as a salesman and brought in Shimon and Joshua as warehouse workers. Joshua loved working with his father. Other than accompany his father to *shul*, Joshua was rarely able to spend time with him. Joshua beamed as he observed his father's quiet dignity and kindness toward his co-workers in the warehouse. He knew of no one as respected and loved in the establishment. Shimon was now fifty-four years old, and in the youth-dominated warehouse he was affectionately called "the old man."

Shimon, however, was not as excited about having Joshua work with him. "I haven't forgotten about his heart defect," Shimon confided in Faige. "I worry about him plenty. I try to do as much lifting for him as I can, but there are times when we all have to unload or load a truck. The other men have caught on, and they also try to help out. We try to give him the cartons to make and let him pack the eggs in them. Sometimes, he helps out packaging butter downstairs because that's the easiest job, but it's boring."

"How does Joshua like the work?" Faige asked.

"He loves it," Shimon replied. "Go figure that out. He's always smiling and singing. The other day he was packaging butter while the intercom was on. Everyone in the office and warehouse heard him singing. When I told him about it later, he wasn't even embarrassed. He just said he hoped they enjoyed it. He's your son, Faige."

"He's your son, too, Shimon," Faige rebutted. "He still goes to college at night and puts on *tefillin* every morning. Do any of the other warehouse men do those things? He's also told me that now that he doesn't have to work on Saturday, he intends to go with you to *shul*. How many of your friends have a twenty-one-year-old son who goes to *shul* with them?"

"None," Shimon admitted proudly.

# CHAPTER 29

★

$\mathcal{I}$n the spring of 1942, the war finally caught up with Joshua. He received his draft notice and at once went to report. That same day he spent the entire afternoon at the Newark Armory being examined and re-examined. Towards evening, he received word that because of his congenital heart condition, he was classified as 4F and would not be drafted.

The military social worker was surprised when he reviewed Joshua's papers. "What are you doing working in the warehouse of a wholesale dairy company when you have a technical background?" he demanded. "You have four years of engineering drawing in high school, and you're attending Newark College of Engineering part-time. That ought to be enough to get you a war job. Here's a possibility that just came across my desk. It's a position with the Westinghouse Elevator Company."

Joshua immediately followed the tip and was hired for a Navy-funded program. The program was responsible for developing a corps of specialists to do stress analysis for the steel work of the deck edge elevators on aircraft carriers.

Joshua was sent to the Newark College of Engineering full-time for ninety days and then was to report to the company in Jersey City. He was paid forty dollars per week while in school and sixty upon his return to Westinghouse. Joshua was unaware that the Navy kept a minority hiring clause so that, as a Jew, he helped the company meet its contractual requirements with the government.

After the initial excitement of attending school and working for the Navy wore off, Joshua found himself depressed over his situation. Most of the men from Joshua's high school class were in uniform. Some had already left for the war in Europe and the Pacific, and others were about to depart. Joshua felt terribly excluded and lonely.

Even his friend Chaim, before he was drafted, had left the Newark area where the two had spent so much time together. It seemed Chaim was in a quandary himself, because he left home without telling Joshua where he was headed. After some indefatigable detective work, he tracked Chaim down to a room on Court Street.

"I've been looking for you for weeks," Joshua said when he found him. "What happened to you?"

"Nothing new," Chaim answered glumly. "It just became obvious that I couldn't live at home any more."

"Why?"

"You know the reasons," Chaim answered. "They haven't changed. I can't live the way my father wants me to, and he won't give up trying to force me. It's easier to live on my own."

Joshua knew the conflicts that continually plagued Chaim's relationship with his father. Chaim was not interested in following in the footsteps of a rabbi. He was constantly rebutting his father's discourses on religious observance and ignoring his admonishments.

"But Jews don't live like that any more," Chaim used to say every time his father would tell him what to do.

"It doesn't matter what other Jews are doing," his father retorted. "What matters is what they should be doing."

Joshua would cringe when he heard their arguments, especially when Chaim's father cited Joshua as an example of someone trying to maintain religious standards. Joshua certainly did not want to come between the two of them, though secretly he often sided with the rabbi's logic.

After Chaim moved, Joshua saw less and less of him until he received a letter, in which Chaim told him he was leaving for active duty the following week. Joshua managed to see him once before he left.

Joshua's friend, Morty, observed Joshua's depression over being on the sidelines. Morty, who was already a chemical engineer, had been hired by a plant in Connecticut to work on producing synthetic rubber, a very high national priority. Morty wasn't released from military service because of a medical disqualification but because of his importance to the war effort.

In an effort to lift his friend's spirits, Morty introduced Joshua to a neighbor of his, Shirley Coppleson. Shirley taught kindergarten in the Union City school system and worked as a part-time buyer in Lowenstein's Dress Shop in downtown Newark. With her friendly, easygoing disposition, Shirley and Joshua hit it off immediately. Though they were both busy during the week, they spent their Sundays together with visits to Coney Island or the Watchung Mountains.

At the end of February of 1943, Joshua reported for work at the Westinghouse Elevator Company in Jersey City. He didn't realize it then, but the date would prove important. It validated the seniority that would fend off many attacks on his job security.

The plant had greatly expanded in order to cope with the

tremendous volume of war orders that were pouring in. Joshua was struck by the size of the plant, which consisted of four nearly contiguous buildings.

Joshua was also taken aback by the atmosphere of his new professional surroundings. He immediately sensed the difference in this world of the non-Jew and instinctively felt that his fellow workers had singled him out, too.

During a speedy tour of the plant, Joshua noticed the knowing glances of the other workers. He overheard one say to another, "These are some of the ninety-day wonders who are going to tell us how to do our jobs. I wonder how many Hebes there are among them."

The less-than-worldly Joshua could not distinguish among gentile ethnicities. Different national origins and religions meant little to him. Originally based in Chicago, Westinghouse had moved its main operation to New Jersey when it bought out the A.B. See Co. in 1937. The Chicago people were mostly white Anglo-Americans, whereas A.B. See had been founded by Swedish Protestants. The two groups largely kept their own council, and each was sure that it stood for the "real" company.

Because of its new Northeast location, many of the new employees were Italian and Irish Catholics, along with a smattering of Jews. It took Joshua a long time to distinguish among these different groups of people.

On his first day at work, the drafting supervisor immediately singled Joshua out. "Is there a Joshua Halevy among you?" he asked.

"Yes, sir," Joshua answered.

"You are to have a different assignment from the rest of the group," the supervisor informed him. "Take the elevator downstairs, and ask for George Socrat's desk. You'll be working with him. He'll explain everything to you."

Joshua was stunned. Why was he being singled out to do

something different? He asked no questions, however, and nervously sought out the elevator.

Joshua's uneasiness was soon quashed. "Pleased to meet you," George Socrat said as he met Joshua. "You're our new draftsman."

"I guess I am," Joshua answered, "but I didn't know it until a few minutes ago. I was hired to do stress analysis for the deck edge elevators."

"That's typical around here," George laughed. "They don't always use people the way they're supposed to. I'm one of the few who is used correctly. John Suozzo—you'll meet him later— and I work on electrical control panels for elevators. In normal times our group would be upwards of fifty people, but in wartime, we're down to three. It's just you, John and me. We work on elevators for defense plants, hospitals, hospital ships and other wartime priorities. Do you object to working with us?"

"Absolutely not," Joshua assured him.

At lunchtime, Bernard Cohen, a former classmate at Newark College, sought Joshua out. "I think you ought to tell the drafting supervisor that you don't want to be separated from the group," Bernard suggested. "After all, you were one of the best students in the class. Why should you train for one job and then have to do another? It doesn't make sense."

"I agree," Joshua answered. "But I really have nothing to complain about. I've done electrical drafting, and I like it. George and Johnny seem okay, and I like the idea of working with a small group."

"Still, if you don't mind my saying," Bernard continued, "I think it smacks of anti-semitism."

"I agree," Joshua said. "Only this time I'm not complaining."

Joshua was quite satisfied with his work. He was assigned a drawing board and a desk adjoining huge windows that afforded a southern exposure. Unlike most of the workers, he often kept the blinds open and sunned himself in his private solarium. Joshua was a serious worker who quickly earned a special rating among his peers. He worked hard, teaching himself elevator electrical drafting and executing the contracts with speed and accuracy.

Joshua also resumed his college education. He decided, upon John's advice, to go to Brooklyn Polytechnical Institute. The school had a complete program in electrical engineering that could be pursued through evening study. Joshua estimated it would take eight years to get a degree.

Joshua's department grew quickly to more than thirty engineers and draftsmen, and Joshua was appointed group leader for geared electrical drafting. He was initially pleased with the new niche; his special value to the department had been officialized. But Joshua could not have known that this attainment was the apex of his upward mobility.

Joshua was eventually ranked as an Associate Engineer, the highest classification possible for an individual without a degree in engineering. But he never became a supervisor. Even his friend John Suozzo, who rose to a very high rung in the company hierarchy, told Joshua, "It's too complicated to make you a supervisor."

Joshua's reaction to that appraisal was clear. He knew it was a classic case of anti-semitism.

Thanks in large part to Joshua's contribution, the Halevy household was able to stabilize during the war years. The family moved to 71 West Runyon Street, where they lived for ten years, their longest stay at a single location.

All through those years, Shimon and Faige tried desperately to get word of their families they had left behind in war-ravaged Europe. Horrible tales of the concentration camps and gas chambers filtered their way into America, leaving relatives scrambling for information that was credible.

It was not until after the war that Shimon and Faige learned how lucky they had been to move to America when they did. From a combined family numbering in the hundreds, perhaps thousands, only a handful had survived.

Shimon's father, Zvi Hersh, who had maintained his dignity, austerity and physical strength till the end, had died right before the war. According to an immigrant to America who had escaped Skalat, Zvi Hersh had died immediately after the Germans invaded Poland. Upon hearing about this dread development, Zvi Hersh apparently told his family, "This is not for me." He then went to his bed and died a natural death, his dreams for his country shredded. He was eighty-six years old.

From Shimon's immediate family, only one nephew, Chana's son, and one niece, Pesya's daughter, who had moved to Israel before the war, survived. Everyone else had perished at the hands of the Nazis. From Faige's family, her sister, Sarah Elfenbein, survived with one daughter, one son and one granddaughter. Two of her brother Eliyahu's sons also survived, one who was drafted into the Russian army and one who made it into the Resistance.

News of the tragedy that had befallen their families devastated Shimon and Faige. Though they were always deprived of a large extended family in America, they were somehow comforted by the knowledge that family did exist elsewhere. Now, however, that was no longer true, and the psychic wounds they suffered when they learned of the bestiality of the crimes committed against their loved ones never completely healed.

Still, Shimon and Faige were thankful for their own lives and even for the daily struggle of survival. Shimon continued to work as a warehouse hand under Jacob's supervision until the mid-Fifties, when Gude and Cole went out of business. Shimon never earned an impressive wage, but that shortcoming was obscured by the extra income brought in by the children living at home.

Ken, as predicted, did very well at the White Rose Tea company. He had become sales manager for the Northeastern area, with his office in New York City. In 1941, Ken's wife Mildred gave birth to a boy, whom they named Zvi Hersh. Ken's second child, a girl named Elaine, was born in 1946.

At that time Ken faced another crossroads. A protege of Jacob's, Lew Isaacson, opened his own wholesale dairy company, hoping to supply the new supermarkets with dairy products. He offered Ken a partnership that required a three-thousand dollar investment. Ken sought advice from his Uncle Jacob.

"Why would you want to go with Lew?" Jacob asked. "You're doing very well at White Rose. Why should you leave?"

"It would be a chance at my own business," Ken answered. "A job, even a good job, can have only limited rewards."

"Don't kid yourself," Jacob said. "I had a business, and it owned me more than I owned it. There is a lot of work and a lot of uncertainty. What do you need it for?"

"It isn't a question of why I need the business," Ken replied. "The question is *how* can I get it? I don't have the three thousand dollars." His words were spoken *soto voce*, and Ken was never sure whether his uncle had heard him or not.

But Ken always regretted his timidity in the face of his uncle. Within a decade, Lew's dairy company had grown to be the largest such enterprise in New Jersey, and Lew became a multimillionaire.

In 1946, Lila went to work for a hearing-aid store that sparked a lifelong interest in hearing aids. She continued working after her marriage to Robert Hersh the following year and opened her own store in 1963.

Morris graduated from South Side High School in January of 1945. He was inducted into the army in April and discharged in 1946 as part of the demobilization that followed World War II. The rather introverted Morris became an accountant after attending New York University and met and married Sydell Levine in December of 1949.

For Joshua, the Forties were among the happiest periods of his life, having begun his job and his relationship with Shirley at about the same time.

Enthused about almost everything, Shirley always heartened and strengthened Joshua with her company. Joshua soon learned that behind the bubbly public personality dwelled a somewhat shy, intelligent, sympathetic nature that captivated him. He marvelled at her ability to attune to his innermost thoughts with empathy and understanding.

Joshua claimed he never proposed to Shirley. It was just assumed they would marry, and the date was set for *Rosh Chodesh Nissan* in 1947. Due to the post-war housing shortage and the large apartment Shirley's parents owned, it was decided the newlyweds would live with them. Their apartment was not far from the Halevy home.

Within a few months, however, the extra strain of the wedding plans combined with her two jobs made Shirley seriously ill. She contracted pneumonia and was confined to bed for almost a month in her parents' house.

Joshua worried considerably about her illness. He found it impossible to keep up with his school work and quit after almost four years of evening study.

But Shirley recovered nicely, and the wedding was joyously held as scheduled. But in June of 1948, barely a year after the wedding, Shirley suffered medical difficulties that mandated major surgery. The doctors projected a full recovery, but as a result of the operation, she would never have children.

# CHAPTER 30

★

*I*n the spring of 1949, Shimon's *shul* chose a new spiritual leader. He was Rabbi Philip Greenstein, who formerly taught Judaism at Notre Dame University. Rabbi Greenstein had originally been hired by the Adas Israel Congregation, where the rabbi shocked the congregation by resigning after only one *Shabbos*. He explained that when he was hired he had been shown a balcony reserved for women but was not told that it was only used during the *Yamim Noraim*. When the synagogue vowed not to change its seating configuration, the rabbi resigned.

The officers of Shimon's congregation, Knesseth Israel, an amalgam of *shuls* that had jointly purchased the former Mendelson building, then proceeded to hire Rabbi Greenstein. The rabbi found their *mechitzah* in order.

The more religious members of Knesseth Israel were most pleased. They had acquired an English-speaking, intellectual rabbi who would be able to communicate with younger people and hopefully win them back to the *shul*.

Joshua was excited. "It's the first time in my life," he told Shirley, "that I hear Torah taught rationally. Other rabbis said things but didn't care if it really made sense. Rabbi Greenstein explains everything he teaches, and he makes everything sound so interesting. The man is brilliant, and he is firm about his convictions."

"Does he respect your convictions?" Shirley asked.

"He never indicates that he disrespects them," Joshua considered. "But he makes no bones about the fact that he wants to teach Torah. He makes it clear that he hopes everyone will listen and change. At least I know where I stand with him."

"What do you mean?" Shirley asked.

"Well, I've been routinely leading the prayers on *Shabbos*. The people love it because they like having someone from the younger generation. But Rabbi Greenstein has stopped me."

Shirley looked surprised. "Why did he do that?"

"Because he said I'm not a *Shabbos* observer."

"But hardly anyone who belongs to that *shul* is a *Shabbos* observer," Shirley pointed out. "So why should that make a difference?"

"He explained that it was just not appropriate," Joshua said, not looking in the least bit offended. "He wasn't picking on me. He was explaining his side. And I don't resent him for it either. As a matter of fact, I even think I agree with him. He's a rather persuasive man, but he's extremely nice, too. He doesn't push his opinions onto anyone."

"I would like to meet him," Shirley said.

"You will," Joshua answered.

"Don't tell me that you are going to make me go to *shul* on *Shabbos*," Shirley laughed.

"No, but how about Friday nights?" Joshua suggested. "Rabbi Greenstein is starting up an *Oneg Shabbos* series after supper on

Friday nights. He spoke to me about it and would like us to come to represent the young people."

Shirley made a face.

"Please, Shirley," Joshua appealed to her. "He's really counting on us to come."

"All right," Shirley sighed, "although I did enjoy my Friday night rest after a week's work."

Joshua and Shirley loved their Friday night get-togethers. Though few other young couples participated, it was Rabbi Greenstein's company they really came for. The rabbi spent hours explaining the reasons behind the customs and *halachos* of Judaism and regaling them with stories of the Torah and Talmud. Much of what the rabbi discussed sounded vaguely familiar to Joshua, though he had never before understood the meaning behind the things he had grown to accept at home.

Rabbi Greenstein also encouraged Joshua and Shirley to visit the Pioneer Hotel in the Catskills, a favorite place of young religious couples in the post-war generation.

"I'm amazed by the scene there," Shirley remarked after their first visit. "In Newark you get the feeling we're out of it. Nobody is interested in being religious except for some old people. Here, young people are as smartly dressed and sophisticated as can be, and they aren't ashamed to be known as religious Jews. I have to say I didn't know young religious people existed until I saw them."

It took Joshua and Shirley almost a year before they became committed *Shomrei Shabbos.* Shimon and Faige were enthusiastic, though a little guilt-ridden at the thought that their son had become religious through an outside source rather than from home. They were too honest, however, to claim a share in the transformation.

But when Joshua began leaving work early on Fridays, Shimon and Faige grew increasingly apprehensive. As the winter months approached, Joshua began coming in earlier on Friday mornings and leaving earlier in the afternoons.

Abjuring work on *Shabbos* carried with it a loss of time-and-a-half pay to Joshua, and it was years before the company allowed him to work overtime in the evenings.

Shimon was extremely fearful of the hourly liberties Joshua was taking, albeit with the permission of Westinghouse. "The boy is risking a job absolutely suited to him over the issue of *Shabbos*," he told Faige.

"Well, you don't work on *Shabbos*," Faige pointed out. "Why are you so upset now that your son doesn't want to either?"

"It's different for his generation," Shimon said. "He's young, and he has great opportunities ahead of him."

The irony of the situation was not lost on Faige. She knew that having Shimon talk to Joshua would be pointless.

"Why don't you go see Rabbi Heschel the Kapichenitzer Rebbe?" she suggested. "He'll know the right thing to do."

Shimon and Joshua went to visit Rabbi Heschel in his house on Henry Street. The rabbi was not moved by Shimon's argument when he presented it to him.

"We're talking about one hour on Fridays and only for the winter months," Shimon appealed to the Rebbe. "I don't think he ought to risk his job for an hour."

"Even one minute of *Shabbos* is holy," Rabbi Heschel answered. "Joshua is doing exactly what has to be done. *Hashem* should help him to be *matzliach*."

And so he was.

In the spring of 1954, Shirley and Joshua bought a house on Vassar Avenue in the Weequahic section of Newark. The new house was three blocks from the Young Israel of Newark and two miles from Shimon's *shul*. It was also near the Hebrew Youth Institution that soon opened up a day school in Newark.

Other signs of Jewish life abounded. A *chassidishe rebbe*, the

Pittsburgher Rebbe, built a large *shul* on Chancellor Avenue, less than a mile from Joshua's new home. The Brisker *shul* under Rabbi Weller also moved to the avenue, and the new YMHA building was on Chancellor Avenue, too. The Beth Israel Hospital was located on Lyons Avenue across the street from the relatively new Young Israel building, and the new *mikveh* was at Lyons and Elizabeth Avenues.

Shortly after Joshua and Shirley moved, they adopted a baby boy, Ephraim Nathan. Ephraim brought with him not only joy but, now that they were a family, a new sense of responsibility and commitment to the couple's Orthodox lifestyle.

Joshua became active in three synagogues from his new home, while still retaining a connection with his father's *shul* and Rabbi Greenstein. The Young Israel had the most influence on the young family. Consisting of four hundred families, it claimed to be the largest Orthodox synagogue in the state. It also occupied an enormous part of Joshua's and Shirley's lives. Joshua became vice-president of the institution from 1959 to 1963 and president from 1963 to 1967, after which he moved his family to Lakewood, New Jersey.

Shirley took charge of the Young Israel kindergarten and nursery school, a paid position. Under her guidance, the school grew from ten to one hundred and thirty children.

Joshua also became involved with the Hebrew Youth Institute, an Agudah-oriented congregation set in place by three rabbis who came to Newark after World War II. The rabbis sought to upgrade Jewish education in Newark and bought a house on Pomona Avenue to use as a *shul* while they drew up plans for a day school.

Joshua was attracted to the religious simplicity of the "boys," as they were often called and occasionally *davened* with them on Pomona Avenue. He befriended one of the rabbis, Rabbi Blumberg. Joshua respected his new companion's untrammeled ardor for Torah education, and Rabbi Blumberg admired Joshua's sincerity.

Their relationship brought about a merger of sorts, and the Hebrew Youth Institute was given use of the Young Israel building for its classes, grades one through four. A five-member Board of Directors was formed to operate the school, consisting of the three founders, the Young Israel's Rabbi Sternman and Joshua. The board agreed to refer any disputes to the *gadol hador*, Rabbi Aharon Kotler of Lakewood.

Unusual for a homegrown Newark boy, the ecumenical Joshua also found himself drawn to the Pittsburgher Rebbe's *shul*. And the Rebbe was interested in Joshua. Why, he thought, is a young man active in Young Israel coming to a *chassidishe shul*?

"How long have you been wearing a *gartel*?" the Rebbe once asked Joshua.

"For a year or so," Joshua answered.

"What were your reasons?" the *Rebbe* gently inquired.

"Probably not the correct ones," Joshua replied. "I think it has more to do with family tradition than religious conviction. My father wears a *gartel*, and so did his father. My maternal grandfather was a *chassidishe* rabbi in Poland, and he wore a *gartel*, too. It just seemed like the right thing for me to continue the practice, because I didn't want the tradition to die out."

The Rebbe did not answer Joshua. He simply kissed him on the forehead.

# CHAPTER 31

★

*I*n 1953, Faige found out that her sister Sarah Elfenbein, who had survived the war with one married daughter and granddaughter, had come to America.

Faige couldn't believe her ears. "My sister here?" she asked exuberantly. "I can't picture her in America. She was the queen of Skalat."

"I'm afraid that there isn't much left to be queen of in Skalat," Shimon replied.

Joshua and Shirley accompanied Faige and Shimon to the New York hotel where the Hebrew Immigrant Assistance Society had found the party temporary shelter. Joshua, who had recently purchased an eight-millimeter motion picture camera, took pictures of the sisters' emotional reunion.

No one present that evening could have imagined that both sisters would be dead within a month. Sarah died of a heart attack only three weeks after she arrived. Faige died on March 6 of congestive heart failure complicated by diabetes and kidney malfunction. She never saw her second granddaughter, born to Morris' wife Sydell, one month later. The new baby was named Frances Anne after Faige Chana.

After Faige's death, Shimon moved in with Lila and Robert in their apartment on Huntington Terrace. He was sixty-seven years old and in poor health. He could not walk without a cane, yet he did not want to stop working. Working kept his mind off his loneliness for Faige.

When his children insisted that his job was too strenuous for him, Shimon came up with an idea. He wanted to open a retail store that would sell eggs. While Ken and Morris received the proposal with raised eyebrows, Joshua and Lila loved the idea.

"I think opening a small store is a great idea," Joshua told Lila. "It'll occupy Dad, and it won't require that much physical work. The only problem is that I don't have the time to really help out. I'll be there whenever I can, but I can't guarantee it will be enough. I don't think Ken or Morris have too much time to spare either."

"Don't worry," Lila reassured him. "Bob's a doll, and he can make his own hours as a salesman, so it won't be a problem. You know, it's funny the way things work out. Mama always said she wouldn't go into business with Papa because he gives everything away. Now that she's gone, he can finally do it."

Joshua laughed. "That's not the only reason Pop is so eager," he said. "Pop has been a frustrated egg candler for almost forty years. Do you know that he wants to build an egg-candling booth and examine the eggs himself before he sells them?"

Lila smiled. "He finally gets the job he wanted."

Sam's Egg Store was successful in every way. He made enough money to offset his generosity, and he had constant company. There were always customers in the store, and Shimon greeted each one by name, promising him the best dozen eggs he could personally candle.

The business lasted seven years. Even after Lila bought a home in Springfield, New Jersey, Bob continued to bring Shimon to the store daily, pursue his own sales route and then return to pick Shimon up in the early evening.

By the mid-Sixties, Shimon was almost completely wheelchair-bound. He had to give up the store and could no longer go to *shul*. Lila took special pains to accommodate her father, who was now residing with her. She built a special bedroom for her father on the ground level of her home with a private bathroom installed just off the family den and not far from the kitchen. Shimon was appreciative but unhappy.

He missed having people around him. Lila was occupied with her hearing-aid store in Springfield, Bob worked all day at sales and little Richard went to school. Shimon was left alone.

One evening Joshua received a telephone call from Lila. "Papa is having a fit. Can you come over right away?"

When Joshua arrived he was surprised to see Jacob already there. Evidently, Shimon still looked to his brother in a crisis.

Shimon was rambling. "I'm not blaming Lila and Bob at all," he said. "They did nothing wrong. They did more than they should have, and I'm grateful. But I can't stay here. I'm going out of my mind."

"Where do you want to go?" Jacob asked. "A man in a wheelchair can't be choosy. Look how beautiful everything is here. You should be proud of your children."

"I am proud of them," Shimon answered. "But I can't stay here."

"So where do you want to go, Pop?" Joshua asked once more.

"One of my friends from the store went to the Ambassador Hotel in Asbury Park," Shimon said. "The hotel caters to people my age. I don't know how much they charge, but that is where I would like to go."

To Shimon's great satisfaction, that is where he went. He ran the hotel *shul* and spent his time sitting in the lobby talking and laughing with the other guests.

Joshua's and Shirley's life also took a turn for the better. In 1961, they adopted their second boy, Aaron Yosef. The family was exultant. Aaron was a source of joy from his first moments as a Halevy. Joshua was also looking forward to the spring of 1963, when he was to graduate from Rutgers University College with a BA in History.

Joshua and Shirley never dreamed these happy events would be marred by an old, recurring problem. During a regular checkup, Shirley's physician discovered another growth and ordered an immediate operation.

Unlike the previous growths, this one was not benign. When the doctor told Joshua the news, he made a decision then that was to last three years. He did not tell Shirley about the true outcome of the surgery and hid the devastating news from the rest of the family as well.

Early in 1966, Shirley began to get severe stomach pains. She was immediately hospitalized and underwent an exploratory operation. The findings were not good. The cancer had spread throughout Shirley's stomach and could not be removed.

But a ray of hope appeared. Shirley's doctor, Dr. Parker, recommended a specialist in chemotherapy. "This a new field that's being used more and more these days in cancer treatment," Dr. Parker explained to Joshua. "The specialist, Dr. Green, says he can help Shirley. I'm not sure it will work, but since we can't come up with anything else, I have requested that he consult with us on your wife."

"She'll be all right," Dr. Green concluded after beginning the treatment. "But I can't tell you for how long."

Shirley left the hospital ten days later. She was terribly weak. The sight of food nauseated her. Joshua tried to be cheerful as he transported her home from the hospital, but Shirley did not want to be consoled. As they left, Joshua saw two nurses huddled in a corner of her room. They were crying.

Shirley was determined, however, to return to her normal routine. After a couple of weeks, Shirley had resumed all her responsibilities, though her chemotherapy treatments left her in a weakened state.

At the same time, Joshua broached Shirley with an idea for change. Some years before, he had gone to Lakewood to meet with Rabbi Aharon Kotler, the *gadol hador*, and discuss plans for the Hebrew day school with which he was involved.

The interview with Rabbi Kotler was an important event for Joshua. He was **well** aware of the honor of speaking with the venerable sage, and he was impressed with how remarkably accessible the Rosh Yeshivah proved to be. The two spoke of the day school with which Joshua was involved and the importance of day school education, which Rabbi Kotler emphasized as paramount to the growth of American Orthodox Jewry. Joshua was amazed with Rabbi Kotler's thorough grasp of the situation and his intricate knowledge of the city's problems and population shifts.

The occasion of Joshua's visit to Rabbi Kotler also afforded him the opportunity of discovering the serene charms of the town of Lakewood. And now, at this crucial juncture in his life, the memories of the lovely town reawakened in his mind.

"I think we should check out Lakewood as a possible place to live," Joshua told Shirley.

Shirley did not disagree that it was time to move out of the Newark area. No one could have imagined how precipitously the Jewish area of Weequahic would wither. From a peak of ninety thousand, the neighborhood's Jewish census skidded to fewer than five thousand in the aftermath of the Newark riots in 1967. Many synagogues in the section reverted to Christian ownership and became Baptist churches. The Temple Bnai Abraham, once an Orthodox and then a Conservative congregation, became the Deliverance Temple, and the Congregation Bnai Jeshurun, built in 1858, became the Hopewell Baptist Church.

But Shirley wasn't sure Lakewood was the right choice. "We don't know anyone there," she said. "Why don't we stay closer to Newark?"

Joshua shook his head. "Maybe what we need is a clean break with a whole new place."

"But Lakewood is very far from Jersey City and Westinghouse," Shirley cautioned. "How would you manage leaving early Friday afternoons in the wintertime?"

"I don't know," Joshua answered, "but first we ought to see if we like the place."

As it turned out, Joshua and Shirley were both impressed with the Lakewood community. A burgeoning religious community, pleasant environment and inexpensive housing quickly convinced the couple of its merits. Only the extended commute to Westinghouse gave Joshua pause, but others had to travel even farther to work, he reasoned.

Joshua and Shirley bought a house at 505 Fourteenth Street in Lakewood. Shirley continued to teach in the public school system, and Joshua commuted to Westinghouse, in addition to taking night classes towards a master's degree in education. It did not take long for the two to become involved in the community, too. A local rabbi in Lakewood had suggested they operate the local school's day camp. Rather than involve themselves in community politics, Joshua and Shirley decided to open a day camp of their own, a project they successfully developed and operated for years.

# CHAPTER 32

★

oshua continued his regular visits to his father from Lakewood. Until his death in September of 1970 at the age of eighty-four, Shimon lived in the Ambassador Hotel, where he refined a stable, inner contentment that helped him abide the strictures of old age. For the last years of his life, he had been virtually immured in a wheelchair, yet he always maintained his cheerful and mild disposition.

After his father's death, Joshua took a year's leave of absence from Westinghouse and secured a teaching job in Staten Island. This way he was able to say *Kaddish* for his father with a *minyan* without jeopardizing work time.

In April of 1971, Joshua's teaching position was discontinued, a victim of the overruling wishes by senior teachers in the city system to work in the desirable Staten Island system. As planned, Joshua went back to work with Westinghouse.

In December of that year, Jacob's wife called Joshua to tell him that his uncle was very ill.

"We'll be over on Sunday," Joshua promised.

Joshua loved his Uncle Jacob, who had been a frequent Sunday visitor when they lived in Newark and who had continued his visits even after the move to Lakewood. For the past few months, however, they hadn't seen Jacob at all.

At their visit, Jacob looked pale and gaunt, and he moved with great difficulty.

"He is dying," his wife told Joshua and Shirley. "Everybody knows it but him. Your uncle has prostate cancer. But even today, if you ask him how he feels, he'll say he's fine. He refuses to talk about being ill."

Jacob spoke of the past instead. "You know," he told Joshua, "I still blame myself for not doing more for you kids."

"Uncle Jacob, how can you say that?" Joshua responded. "You saved my family twice, not once. Didn't you bring my father to this country two times?"

"I know," Jacob said. "I did a lot, but I could've done more."

"That's nonsense," Joshua insisted. "We all went to you when we really had to. Didn't I go to you in 1939 after I graduated from high school? You helped me then. You know, Uncle Jacob, you're a much better uncle than I am. I hardly see my nephews and nieces. They're scattered all over New Jersey."

But Jacob shook his head and looked past Joshua. After so many years, Joshua knew his uncle was not a person who was easily persuaded. And he never forgot his mother's antagonistic feelings towards her brother-in-law, though they were rarely spoken in front of him.

The following week, Joshua attended Jacob's funeral. After Jacob's death, his wife opened Jacob's safe deposit box and found many scraps of paper. They were IOUs from different members of the Gross family in varying amounts. The notes had never been repaid. Apparently, Jacob had not asked that they be redeemed.

It seemed Joshua would not be spared from grief that year. In the spring of 1973, Shirley's cancer, which had remained in remission for seven years due to the chemotherapy, resurfaced.

After a series of hospitalizations, she was brought to Mount Sinai at the end of March for what was to be the last time. For three weeks, Shirley's body strove for equilibrium. She was completely alert and talked easily but soberly. She knew how sick she was.

After she died, the nurse in her room called Joshua over. "I thought you would want to know what Shirley's last words were," she said. "Right before she died, Shirley called out in a loud clear voice, 'Joshua, Joshua, Joshua!'"

Joshua was broken by his loss, yet he knew he had to recover the peace of mind to gear him for his larger responsibilities. Ephraim was now twenty, and Aaron was twelve. Both of them had only Joshua to rely on emotionally and financially.

Before her death, Shirley had contributed forty percent of the Halevy budget. Now Joshua had to accept overtime work in order to bridge the new deficit. Yet by so doing, he was kept from his children for a longer time during the day, thus depriving them of leadership and companionship when they needed it most.

Joshua's neighbors, the Levines, did uncommon kindnesses to the bereft family, claiming the Halevys as virtual permanent *Shabbos* guests and telephoning with touching frequency with offers of help.

Not long after, Westinghouse decided to move the elevator division from Jersey City to Gettysburg, Pennsylvania, and Randolph, New Jersey. Early retirement, long a possibility for Joshua, now became a necessity. Joshua did not seek to move to either location. He would be eligible for retirement at age fifty-eight in 1979. At that time Joshua planned to retire and rely on his pension and prospective teaching income for support.

In January of 1974, a local rabbi of a nearby *shul* introduced Joshua to a widow named Sarah Cohen who lived in Long Branch.

"She lost her husband this past August," the rabbi told Joshua. "She's a wonderful lady, and she has two grown children, a boy and a girl."

Sarah was indeed a lovely and compassionate person, and her relationship with Joshua blossomed. They became engaged in May and married in September.

The following year, Joshua embarked on a pursuit of a dream he had had for years. He enrolled in a doctorate program in education.

"Shirley and I always had this idea of a two-teacher family," Joshua explained to Sarah. "But it always somehow eluded us. I don't want this opportunity to pass me by."

"And what do you propose to write your dissertation about?" Sarah inquired.

"I'd like it to be on Jewish education," Joshua answered right away.

"That's a broad topic," Sarah said.

Joshua nodded his head. "You're right," he agreed. "What I specifically had in mind was Beth Medrash Govoha of Lakewood. I think it's a remarkable example of the development of Jewish Orthodoxy in this country."

Joshua decided to discuss the subject with Rabbi Shneur Kotler, and he enthusiastically introduced the Rosh Yeshivah to his dissertation idea. "I will start with Rav Aharon, *zatzal*," Joshua explained, "and trace his education, from the Slobodka Yeshivah in Europe to America. I think that the story of the *yeshivah* will in a very large way be the story of Rav Aharon."

Rav Shneur was quickly taken with the idea and heartily approved of Joshua's using the *yeshivah* as the subject of an English dissertation at Rutger's University. He even gave him books and pamphlets and offered to help with any information Joshua might need.

It took Joshua several years to complete his writing, which sought to articulate the philosophy of the *yeshivah* with its European, *mussar*-grounded roots. The work excited both him and ultimately his counselor at the university.

"This stuff is much more interesting than statistics," the gentile newcomer to the *yeshivah* world remarked.

Several weeks after sending a copy of the dissertation to Rabbi Kotler, Joshua visited the Rosh Yeshivah once again in search of a *haskamah* from a *gadol* in Torah.

"Did the Rosh Yeshivah have a chance to read the material?" Joshua asked.

"Yes," Rabbi Kotler answered.

"Does the Rosh Yeshivah approve?" Joshua asked timidly.

"Well, there is nothing of which to disapprove," Rav Shneur said. "When you're talking about *mussar* and *yeshivos*, what can be bad? I read most of it, but the Rebbetzin has read the entire book. She wants to talk to you about it. I'll call her up."

"How did the Rebbetzin like my book?" Joshua asked the Rebbetzin.

"I enjoyed reading the material very much," came the immediate reply.

"I think I did a service to the *yeshivah*," Joshua said.

"And to all of Klal Yisrael," the Rebbetzin answered.

Joshua smiled and thanked Rabbi Kotler and his Rebbetzin. But when he left the Rosh Yeshivah, he wasn't thinking about his dissertation. He was thinking about a little boy growing up in Newark, New Jersey, who had never attended a *yeshivah* at all.

More than a half-century of his own family history flashed through his mind—the convulsions of Europe that had uprooted his family and deposited them on the shores of America; the gilded American dreams that had driven them and countless others like them to sacrifice and toil for a better tomorrow; the terrible spiritual price that most of the immigrants had paid for a share in the American dream; and the ultimate realization that material success did not necessarily bring happiness and contentment.

Yet Joshua was encouraged by the knowledge that Judaism had been so deeply imbedded in his family by his ancestors that an indestructible seed remained in spite of the years and decades of drift. In his own heart, that seed had bloomed and blossomed and developed into a burning love for the Torah and all aspects of Jewish life. Perhaps that was the true fulfillment of his American dream, the freedom to live in security and dignity according to one's own beliefs, to work for a better future but always to cherish the past.

*Tzvi Hersh
Halevy*

*Shimon
Halevy*

*Joshua Halevy*

# GLOSSARY

★

**aliyah:** honorary post at the Torah reading
**aron:** ark
**bar-mitzvah:** *halachic* adulthood
**bimah:** pulpit
**bris:** covenant
**challah:** *Shabbos* loaves
**Chanukah:** Festival of Lights
**chassidishe:** relating to *chassidus*
**chazan:** cantor
**cheder:** elementary Torah school
**chevrah kaddisha:** burial society
**chupah:** bridal canopy
**daven:** pray
**galus:** exile
**gartel:** prayer sash
**goyim:** gentiles
**halachos:** Jewish laws
**haskamah:** approbation
**Kaddish:** mourner's prayer
**kiddush:** sanctification of *Shabbos* or festivals
**kugel:** pudding [Yiddish]

**mazel tov:** congratulations
**mechitzah:** partition
**mezuzah:** scroll on doorpost
**mikveh:** ritual bath
**Minchah:** afternoon service
**minyan:** quorum of ten
**mitzvah:** Torah commandment
**mussar:** ethical instruction
**parshah:** portion of the Torah
**payos:** earlocks
**Pesach:** Passover
**Purim:** Festival of Lots
**rebbe:** *chassidic* rabbi
**Rosh Hashanah:** New Year
**rosh yeshivah:** dean
**schnapps:** liquor
**sefer:** book
**sefer Torah:** Torah scroll
**Shabbos:** the Sabbath
**Shacharis:** morning prayers
**shammash:** beadle
**sheitel:** wig
**sheva berachos:** the seven nuptial blessings

**shochet:** ritual slaughterer
**shofar:** ram's horn
**shomer Shabbos:** *Shabbos*
   observer
**shtetl:** village
**shtreimel:** *chassidic* headdress
**shul:** synagogue
**siddur:** prayer book
**simchah:** rejoicing

**Sukkos:** Festival of Tabernacles
**tallis:** prayer shawl
**tefillin:** phylacteries
**tzeddakah:** charity
**Yamim Noraim:** Days of Awe
**yeshivah:** Torah school
**Yom Kippur:** Day of Atonement
**Yom Tov:** festival